The Comprehensive

NINJA FOODI XL PRO

AIR FRYER OVEN

COOKBOOK

OVER 200 EASY AND MOUTHWATERING RECIPES TO FEED YOUR FAMILY HEALTHY WITH YOUR NINJA FOODI XL PRO AIR FRY OVEN

DAMIAN STRICKLAND

CONTENTS

RECIPE INDEX

INTRODUCTION

What Is the Ninja Foodi XL Pro Air Fryer Oven

Air fryer toaster ovens are standard toaster ovens with the air frying function. Besides toasting, baking, and defrosting, they can also produce crispy, crunchy fries as well as a solely-dedicated air fryer.

Built with even-heat distributing convection technology, the best air fryer toaster ovens come with the advantage of promoting faster cooking times while still producing crisp fried food without the added oil. In this way they can reduce the fat content of fried foods by up to 95%. If you love French fries, but try to stay away from deep-fried foods as much as possible, this kitchen appliance can satisfy your craving.

Air fryer toaster ovens could certainly help you to avoid excess weight gain, and create healthier eating habits. They can also help you save a lot of cooking time, effort, and energy consumption, offering you a more efficient way to improve your culinary experience.

We found that air fryer toaster ovens can even produce cripier, more evenly fried food than some pod-shaped air fryers. They also come with more useful accessories to meet your air frying and baking needs. If you're dealing with a tiny kitchen, where space is at a premium for both an air fryer and toaster oven, the combo models are the best solution for effectively managing your space constraints.

Having less stuff around could also allow for a greater freedom in the design of your kitchen, making it easier to remodel or rearrange your kitchen.

Advantages of Your Ninja Foodi XL Pro Air Fryer Oven

1.   Circulation technology

The Air Fryer's high-speed air circulation technology allows you to make delicious Chips with up to 80% less fat than traditional electric fryers! The unique combination of fast circulating hot air and oven components will enable you to fry various delicious food, snacks, seafood, and more quickly and easily. Because you only use air frying, it produces less odor and steam than conventional frying and is easy to clean in everyday use, making it both safe and economical!

2.   Temperature control

Allows you to preset the optimum cooking temperature for your food up to 200 degrees. Enjoy golden-colored crispy fries, snacks, chicken, and meat at the right temperature for optimum results!

3.   Small footprint

A large oven can take up a lot of space if you don't have a large kitchen, but an air fryer is usually slightly larger than a rice cooker, making it very easy to move around.

4.   No oil consumption

It's easy to make 1-2 servings of food, so you can fry as much as you like, unlike real deep-fried food, which uses so much oil that you have to fry a lot of it, and it doesn't taste good if you don't destroy it right away.

5.   No worries about cleaning

Once the air fryer has cooled down, douse the inside of the pan under water or wipe it with a clean rag. Isn't the air fryer much easier to clean than other pots and pans?

6.   Control system to save time and effort

The air fryer has a control system. Except for the first few minutes when you need to shake the frying basket, there is no need for supervision after that. When the temperature is too high, it automatically adjusts so that there is no scorching. The air fryer stops automatically when the time is right.

7.   **Less oil consumption and no loss of taste**

This type of cooker uses air circulating at high speed to produce a factor that acts on the ingredients so that they can be crisped quickly, and the oil in them can be fried out so that the fat in the ingredients is reduced.

Three Tips for Your Ninja Foodi XL Pro Air Fryer Oven Cooking Results

Just like any form of cooking, air frying can be an art form. Use these helpful tips to make sure your meal turns out perfectly browned and crisp every time.

1.   Don't overload the pan or tray. If ingredients are packed too close together, the hot air won't be able to reach all the edges and create that perfect fried crispiness.
2.   Double-check your recipe. The proper cooking time and the temperature are essential for the best air fryer oven results. Also, make sure you are using the correct amount of oil. With no oil, food will not be as crisp, and the texture can turn gritty, but too much oil and food can turn out soggy. Be sure to use cooking oils or sprays that can stand up to high temperatures like avocado, grape seed, and peanut oils.
3.   Use the correct tray, which lets air circulate around each piece of food, creating quicker, crispier results. When using the Air Fry Tray, put a baking sheet on a rack or two below it. This keeps drips and crumbs from landing on the oven bottom, where they can burn and create smoke. For additional protection, place some foil-lined parchment paper on the baking sheet.

Effective Methods for Cleaning the Ninja Foodi XL Pro Air Fryer Oven

If you've got a bathtub or a large enough basin to submerge your oven racks, this might be the easiest and most effective way to clean them because you don't have to do much! The cleaning solution used to soak the racks will help loosen up grime and even cut through burnt-on grease, making it far easier to scrub down after.

Here is the step-by-step soaking method to clean oven racks with vinegar.

Step 1: Apply Baking Soda and Vinegar

These two ingredients are a match made in heaven when it comes to household cleaning. It is particularly effective in removing grease and burnt stains from metal surfaces including stainless steel pots and pans. To use this method when cleaning oven racks, sprinkle some baking soda around the tub, place the racks down and sprinkle more of the powder so that both sides can be cleaned efficiently; pour raw vinegar over the racks and allow science to take over! You will start to see the ingredients bubble and foam; that's exactly what you want.

After this bubbling process dies down, pour hot water over the racks to submerge them. Although it's typically advised to leave them to soak overnight, a minimum of four hours should be enough to clean your oven racks effectively.

Step 2: Scrub Them Down

By now, most of the grime will be removable with just a quick wipe, however, thorough scrubbing is advised, particularly for those tricky corners. Start by using a regular scrubber to clean the oven racks, one grid line at a time. Observe each corner as you go; if your scrubber isn't doing a good enough job at getting grease or grime out, switch to a narrow cleaning brush or an old clean toothbrush.

Step 3: Rinse and Dry

Once you're satisfied with the scrubbing, it's time to rinse off all the grime and cleaning solution. Do this under running water and, again, pay attention to corners to ensure that no grime gets left behind. After rinsing the racks, leave them to air dry or wipe with a clean kitchen towel before replacing them.

BREAKFAST

Mushroom Blue Cheese Crostini

Servings: 10
Cooking Time: 3 Minutes

Ingredients:

- 1 tablespoon olive oil
- 8 ounces mushrooms, wild or button, sliced
- 3 cloves garlic, minced
- 2 tablespoons fresh flat-leaf (Italian) parsley, minced
- 2 teaspoons chopped fresh thyme, rosemary, or sage leaves
- Kosher salt and freshly ground black pepper
- 10 to 12 country bread, artisan bread, or baguette slices
- 1 cup grated fontina cheese
- ½ cup blue cheese or Gorgonzola crumbles
- 1 tablespoon fresh lemon juice
- Whole flat-leaf (Italian) parsley, for garnish

Directions:

1. Heat the olive oil in a medium nonstick skillet over medium-high heat. Add the mushrooms and cook, stirring frequently, until the liquid has evaporated, 7 to 10 minutes. Add the garlic and cook for 1 minute. Remove from the heat. Stir in the parsley and thyme and season with salt and pepper. Allow the mixture to cool.
2. Toast the slices of bread in the toaster oven.
3. Stir the fontina and blue cheese into the mushroom mixture.
4. Preheat the toaster oven on 400°F. Arrange the toasted baguette slices on a 12 x 12-inch baking sheet. Distribute the mushroom cheese mixture evenly over the toasted bread slices. Broil until the cheese melts, 2 to 3 minutes. Drizzle with the lemon juice. Garnish each crostini with a parsley leaf. Serve immediately.

Turkey And Tuna Melt

Servings: 2
Cooking Time: 4 Minutes

Ingredients:

- 4 slices multigrain bread Spicy brown mustard
- 1 6-ounce can tuna in water, drained well and crumbled
- ¼ pound thinly sliced turkey breast
- 4 slices low-fat Monterey Jack cheese
- 2 tablespoons finely chopped scallions
- Salt and freshly ground black pepper

Directions:

1. Spread one side of each bread slice with mustard and place on an oiled or nonstick
2. 6½ × 10-inch baking sheet.
3. Layer 2 slices with equal portions of tuna, turkey, cheese, and scallion. Season to taste with salt and pepper.
4. TOAST twice, or until the cheese is melted.

Southern-style Biscuits

Servings: 10
Cooking Time: 12 Minutes

Ingredients:

- 2 cups all-purpose flour
- 1 tablespoon baking powder
- 1 teaspoon table salt
- 4 tablespoons cold, unsalted butter, cut into bits
- ¾ to 1 cup buttermilk

Directions:

1. Preheat the toaster oven to 450 ºF.

2. Combine the flour, baking powder, and salt in a large bowl. Using a pastry cutter or two knives, cut the butter into the flour mixture until the mixture is crumbly throughout. Pour in the buttermilk and gently mix until just combined.

3. Turn the dough onto a lightly floured surface and knead lightly about 8 times. Roll the dough, using a rolling pin, until about ½ inch thick. Cut out rounds using a 2 ½ -inch cutter. Place on an ungreased 12 x 12-inch baking pan or 8-inch round pan.

4. Bake for 10 to 12 minutes or until golden brown. Let cool slightly before serving warm.

Hashbrown Potatoes Lyonnaise

Servings: 4
Cooking Time: 33 Minutes

Ingredients:

- 1 Vidalia (or other sweet) onion, sliced
- 1 teaspoon butter, melted
- 1 teaspoon brown sugar
- 2 large russet potatoes (about 1 pound), sliced ½-inch thick
- 1 tablespoon vegetable oil
- salt and freshly ground black pepper

Directions:

1. Preheat the toaster oven to 370°F.

2. Toss the sliced onions, melted butter and brown sugar together in the air fryer oven. Air-fry for 8 minutes, help the onions cook evenly.

3. While the onions are cooking, bring a 3-quart saucepan of salted water to a boil on the stovetop. Par-cook the potatoes in boiling water for 3 minutes. Drain the potatoes and pat them dry with a clean kitchen towel.

4. Add the potatoes to the onions in the air fryer oven and drizzle with vegetable oil. Toss to coat the potatoes with the oil and season with salt and freshly ground black pepper.

5. Increase the air fryer oven temperature to 400°F and air-fry for 22 minutes tossing the vegetables a few times during the cooking time to help the potatoes brown evenly. Season to taste again with salt and freshly ground black pepper and serve warm.

Cherry Almond Scones

Servings: 12
Cooking Time: 25 Minutes

Ingredients:

- 2 3/4 cups all-purpose flour
- 1/2 cup sugar
- 1 tablespoon baking powder
- 3/4 teaspoon salt
- 1 cup dried cherries
- 1 cup slivered almonds
- 1/2 cup cold butter, sliced into tablespoons
- 2 large eggs
- 1/2 cup sour cream
- 1 teaspoon almond extract
- 1/2 teaspoon vanilla extract
- 1 tablespoon milk
- Coarse sugar

Directions:

1. Preheat the toaster oven to 375°F.

2. In a large mixer bowl, stir flour, sugar, baking powder and salt until blended.

3. Add butter pieces. Beat on MEDIUM speed until mixture is crumbly with some larger pieces of butter.

4. In a large mixer bowl on MEDIUM-HIGH speed, beat eggs, sour cream, almond extract and vanilla extract until blended.

5. Stir into flour mixture until mixture is blended and no longer dry. Lightly knead in cherries and almonds.

6. Divide dough in half. Form each into circles about 3/4-inch thick on parchment-lined baking sheet.

7. Brush each circle with milk and sprinkle tops with coarse sugar. Using a floured metal spatula, cut each circle into 6 wedges. Separate the wedges, leaving 1/2-inch between each wedge.

8. Bake for 20 to 25 minutes or until golden brown. Cool for 15 minutes before serving.

Bacon Chicken Ranch Sandwiches

Servings: 2
Cooking Time: 23 Minutes

Ingredients:

- Nonstick cooking spray
- ½ pound chicken tenders (about 4)
- 4 slices country or sourdough bread
- 2 tablespoons unsalted or salted butter, softened
- 2 tablespoons ranch dressing
- 2 slices sliced Colby Jack or cheddar cheese
- 6 slices bacon, cooked until crisp

Directions:

1. Preheat the toaster oven to 375°F. Spray a small baking sheet with nonstick cooking spray.

2. Place the chicken tenders on the prepared baking sheet. Bake, uncovered, for 12 to 15 minutes or until the chicken is done and a meat thermometer registers 165°F. Carefully remove from the oven and allow the chicken tenders to cool slightly.

3. Increase the toaster oven temperature to 450°F. Place a 12 x 12-inch baking pan in the toaster oven while it is preheating.

4. Spread one side of each slice of bread with butter. Place two pieces of bread, buttered side down, on a sheet of parchment or wax paper. Spread each slice with 1 tablespoon ranch dressing. Divide the chicken tenders among the two slices. Cut the cheese to fit on the chicken tenders and within the bread perimeter. Fold the slices of bacon to fit within the bread perimeter. Top with the second slice of bread, butter side up.

5. Carefully remove the hot baking pan from the toaster oven and place the sandwiches on the baking sheet. Place the baking sheet in the toaster oven and bake for 4 minutes. Carefully remove the pan and flip the sandwich, using a spatula. Bake for an additional 3 to 4 minutes, or until the sandwich is golden brown and the cheese is melted.

6. Cool slightly and cut in half for serving.

Buttered Poppy Seed Bread

Servings: 6
Cooking Time: 25 Minutes

Ingredients:

- 3 tablespoons unsalted butter, melted
- 1 (1-pound) loaf frozen white bread dough
- 1 teaspoon poppy seeds
- ¼ teaspoon onion powder
- ¼ teaspoon garlic powder
- ¼ teaspoon freshly ground black pepper

Directions:

1. Pour about half of the melted butter into a 9 x 5-inch loaf pan. Brush the butter to cover the

sides and bottom of the pan. Place the frozen bread loaf in the pan. Brush the top of the loaf with the remaining butter, covering completely. Stir the poppy seeds, onion powder, garlic powder, and pepper in a small bowl. Sprinkle the seasonings over the top of the bread. Cover with plastic wrap and refrigerate overnight.

2. Remove the bread from the refrigerator and loosen the plastic wrap so it is loosely covered. Let it rise at room temperature until the top of the bread is just over the top edge of the pan, about 2 to 4 hours.

3. Preheat the toaster oven to 350°F.

4. Bake for 20 to 25 minutes or until the bread is golden brown.

5. Let cool for 5 minutes, then remove the loaf from the pan and place on a wire rack to cool for a few minutes. Slice and serve warm.

Brunch Burritos

Servings: 4
Cooking Time: 14 Minutes

Ingredients:
- Egg mixture:
- 4 medium eggs, lightly beaten
- 3 tablespoons finely chopped bell pepper
- 2 tablespoons finely chopped onion
- 4 strips lean turkey bacon, uncooked and cut into small ¼ × ¼-inch pieces
- 1 tablespoon chopped fresh cilantro
- ½ teaspoon ground cumin
- ½ teaspoon chili powder
- Salt and red pepper flakes to taste
- 4 6-inch flour tortillas
- 4 tablespoons salsa
- 4 tablespoons shredded part-skim, low-moisture mozzarella

Directions:
1. Combine the egg mixture ingredients in an oiled or nonstick 8½ × 8½ × 2-inch square baking (cake) pan.

2. TOAST twice, or until the mixture is firm and cooked.

3. Spoon the egg mixture in equal portions onto the center of each tortilla. Add 1 tablespoon salsa and 1 tablespoon mozzarella cheese to each. Roll each tortilla around the filling and lay, seam side down, in an oiled or nonstick 8½ × 8½ × 2-inch square baking (cake) pan.

4. BROIL for 8 minutes, or until lightly browned.

Mushroom-spinach Frittata With Feta

Servings: 4
Cooking Time: 35 Minutes

Ingredients:
- 1 tablespoon olive oil
- 1 cup white mushrooms, chopped
- 1 shallot, finely chopped
- 1 teaspoon minced garlic
- 4 large eggs
- ½ cup milk
- ½ cup fresh baby spinach, shredded
- 1 tablespoon fresh basil, chopped
- ⅛ teaspoon sea salt
- ⅛ teaspoon freshly ground black pepper
- ¾ cup feta cheese, crumbled

Directions:
1. Place the baking tray on position 1 and preheat the toaster oven on BAKE to 350°F for 5 minutes.

2. Add the oil to an 8-inch-square baking dish, tilting the dish to coat the bottom.

3. Combine the mushrooms, shallot, and garlic in the baking dish. Bake the vegetables for 5 minutes or until softened, stirring halfway through.

4. While the vegetables are cooking, in a large bowl, whisk the eggs, milk, spinach, basil, salt, and pepper.

5. Take the baking dish out of the oven and pour in the egg mixture, stirring slightly to evenly disperse the vegetables.

6. Top the frittata with the feta cheese and bake for 30 minutes. The frittata should be puffy and golden, and a knife inserted in the center should come out clean.

7. Cool for 5 minutes and serve.

Make-ahead Currant Cream Scones

Servings: 8

Cooking Time: 60 Minutes

Ingredients:

- 2 cups (10 ounces) all-purpose flour
- 3 tablespoons sugar
- 1 tablespoon baking powder
- ½ teaspoon table salt
- 5 tablespoons unsalted butter, cut into ¼-inch pieces and chilled
- ½ cup dried currants
- 1 cup heavy cream

Directions:

1. Adjust toaster oven rack to middle position and preheat the toaster oven to 375 degrees. Line large and small rimmed baking sheets with parchment paper.

2. Process flour, sugar, baking powder, and salt in food processor until combined, about 6 seconds. Scatter butter over top and pulse until mixture resembles coarse cornmeal with some slightly larger butter lumps, about 12 pulses. Transfer mixture to large bowl and stir in currants. Stir in cream with rubber spatula until dough begins to form, about 30 seconds.

3. Turn dough and any floury bits onto lightly floured counter and knead until rough, slightly sticky ball forms, 5 to 10 seconds. Shape dough into 8-inch round, about ¾ inch thick. Cut dough into 8 wedges.

4. Space desired number of scones at least 1 inch apart on prepared small sheet; space remaining scones evenly on prepared large sheet. Bake small sheet of scones until scone tops are light golden brown, 18 to 23 minutes. Transfer scones to wire rack and let cool for at least 10 minutes before serving.

5. Freeze remaining large sheet of scones until firm, about 1 hour. Transfer scones to 1-gallon zipper-lock bag and freeze for up to 1 month. To bake frozen scones, increase baking time to 20 to 25 minutes; do not thaw.

Strawberry Toast

Servings: 4

Cooking Time: 8 Minutes

Ingredients:

- 4 slices bread, ½-inch thick
- butter-flavored cooking spray
- 1 cup sliced strawberries
- 1 teaspoon sugar

Directions:

1. Spray one side of each bread slice with butter-flavored cooking spray. Lay slices sprayed side down.

2. Divide the strawberries among the bread slices.

3. Sprinkle evenly with the sugar and place in the air fryer oven in a single layer.

4. Air-fry at 390°F for 8 minutes. The bottom should look brown and crisp and the top should look glazed.

Morning Glory Muffins

Servings: 6

Cooking Time: 25 Minutes

Ingredients:

- Oil spray (hand-pumped)
- ¼ cup raisins
- 1 cup whole-wheat flour
- ½ cup packed dark brown sugar
- 1 teaspoon baking soda
- 1¼ teaspoons pumpkin pie spice
- ¼ teaspoon sea salt
- 1 cup carrot, finely shredded
- 1 small apple, peeled, cored, and shredded
- ⅓ cup shredded, sweetened coconut
- 2 large eggs
- ¼ cup canola oil
- Juice and zest of ½ orange

Directions:

1. Place the rack on position 1 and preheat the toaster oven on BAKE to 350°F for 5 minutes. Lightly spray 6 muffin cups with the oil or line them with paper liners.

2. In a small bowl, cover the raisins with hot water and set aside.

3. In a large bowl, whisk the flour, brown sugar, baking soda, pumpkin pie spice, and salt. Add the carrot, apple, and coconut, and toss to mix.

4. In a small bowl, beat the eggs, oil, orange juice, and orange zest.

5. Drain the raisins, squeezing out as much water as possible.

6. Add the wet ingredients and raisins to the dry ingredients and mix until the batter is just combined.

7. Spoon the batter into the muffin cups.

8. Bake for 25 minutes or until a knife inserted in the center comes out clean.

9. Remove from the oven and let cool before serving.

Roasted Vegetable Frittata

Servings: 1

Cooking Time: 19 Minutes

Ingredients:

- ½ red or green bell pepper, cut into ½-inch chunks
- 4 button mushrooms, sliced
- ½ cup diced zucchini
- ½ teaspoon chopped fresh oregano or thyme
- 1 teaspoon olive oil
- 3 eggs, beaten
- ½ cup grated Cheddar cheese
- salt and freshly ground black pepper, to taste
- 1 teaspoon butter
- 1 teaspoon chopped fresh parsley

Directions:

1. Preheat the toaster oven to 400°F.

2. Toss the peppers, mushrooms, zucchini and oregano with the olive oil and air-fry for 6 minutes, redistribute the ingredients once or twice during the cooking process.

3. While the vegetables are cooking, beat the eggs well in a bowl, stir in the Cheddar cheese and season with salt and freshly ground black pepper. Add the air-fried vegetables to this bowl when they have finished cooking.

4. Place a 6- or 7-inch non-stick metal cake pan into the air fryer oven with the butter using an

aluminum sling to lower the pan into the air fryer oven. (Fold a piece of aluminum foil into a strip about 2-inches wide by 24-inches long.) Air-fry for 1 minute at 380°F to melt the butter. Remove the cake pan and rotate the pan to distribute the butter and grease the pan. Pour the egg mixture into the cake pan and return the pan to the air fryer oven, using the aluminum sling.

5. Air-fry at 380°F for 12 minutes, or until the frittata has puffed up and is lightly browned. Let the frittata sit in the air fryer oven for 5 minutes to cool to an edible temperature and set up. Remove the cake pan from the air fryer oven, sprinkle with parsley and serve immediately.

Cheddar Bacon Broiler

Servings: 4
Cooking Time: 8 Minutes

Ingredients:
- 4 slices pumpernickel bread
- 4 strips lean turkey bacon, cut in half
- 4 tablespoons shredded Cheddar cheese
- 4 tablespoons grated Parmesan cheese
- 4 tablespoons finely chopped bell pepper
- 1 medium tomato, chopped
- 2 tablespoons finely chopped onion
- Salt and freshly ground black pepper
- 2 tablespoons chopped fresh parsley or cilantro

Directions:
1. Layer the bread slices with 2 half strips turkey bacon and 1 tablespoon each Cheddar cheese, Parmesan cheese, and bell pepper. Sprinkle each with equal portions of tomato and onion. Season to taste with salt and pepper.
2. BROIL on a broiling rack with a pan underneath for 8 minutes, or until the cheese is well melted. Before serving, sprinkle with parsley or cilantro.

Breakfast Banana Bread

Servings: 6
Cooking Time: 40 Minutes

Ingredients:
- 2 ripe bananas
- 1 egg
- ½ cup skim milk
- 2 tablespoons honey
- 1 tablespoon vegetable oil
- 1 cup unbleached flour
- ¾ cup chopped trail mix
- 1 teaspoon baking powder
- Salt

Directions:
1. Preheat the toaster oven to 400° F.
2. Process the bananas, egg, milk, honey, and oil in a blender or food processor until smooth and transfer to a mixing bowl.
3. Add the flour and trail mix, stirring to mix well. Add the baking powder and stir just enough to blend it into the batter. Add salt to taste. Pour the mixture into an oiled or nonstick 4½ × 8½ × 2¼-inch loaf pan.
4. BAKE for 40 minutes, or until a toothpick inserted in the center comes out clean.

Breakfast Blueberry Peach Crisp

Servings: 8
Cooking Time: 60 Minutes

Ingredients:
- Filling Ingredients
- 4 cups blueberries, fresh or frozen
- 2 cups peaches, sliced
- 1 teaspoon vanilla extract

- 2 teaspoons lemon juice
- 4 tablespoons pure maple syrup
- 1½ tablespoons cornstarch
- A tiny pinch of salt
- Topping Ingredients
- 2½ cups rolled oats
- 5 tablespoons almond meal (or almond flour)
- 1 teaspoon cinnamon
- 5 tablespoons pure maple syrup
- 3 tablespoons coconut sugar (or brown sugar)
- 7 tablespoons coconut oil, melted
- 1 cup sliced almonds
- 1 cup chopped walnuts
- ¼ teaspoon salt

Directions:

1. Combine the blueberries, peaches, vanilla extract, lemon juice, maple syrup, cornstarch, and salt in a bowl and toss to combine. Pour mixture into the baking dish.
2. Combine all the topping ingredients in a separate bowl and stir until clumps form, then spread evenly over the fruit mixture.
3. Preheat the toaster Oven to 350°F.
4. Place the baking dish on the wire rack, then insert rack at low position in the preheated oven.
5. Select the Bake function, adjust time to 1 hour, then press
6. Start/Pause.
7. Remove crisp when golden on top and fruit is bubbly.
8. Serve with yogurt for breakfast or vanilla ice cream for dessert.

Fry Bread

Servings: 4
Cooking Time: 5 Minutes

Ingredients:

- 1 cup flour
- 2 teaspoons baking powder
- ¼ teaspoon salt
- ¼ cup lukewarm milk
- 1 teaspoon oil
- 2–3 tablespoons water
- oil for misting or cooking spray

Directions:

1. Stir together flour, baking powder, and salt. Gently mix in the milk and oil. Stir in 1 tablespoon water. If needed, add more water 1 tablespoon at a time until stiff dough forms. Dough shouldn't be sticky, so use only as much as you need.
2. Divide dough into 4 portions and shape into balls. Cover with a towel and let rest for 10 minutes.
3. Preheat the toaster oven to 390°F.
4. Shape dough as desired:
5. a. Pat into 3-inch circles. This will make a thicker bread to eat plain or with a sprinkle of cinnamon or honey butter. You can cook all 4 at once.
6. b. Pat thinner into rectangles about 3 x 6 inches. This will create a thinner bread to serve as a base for dishes such as Indian tacos. The circular shape is more traditional, but rectangles allow you to cook 2 at a time in your air fryer oven.
7. Spray both sides of dough pieces with oil or cooking spray.
8. Place the 4 circles or 2 of the dough rectangles in the air fryer oven and air-fry at 390°F for 3 minutes. Spray tops, turn, spray other side, and air fry for 2 more minutes. If necessary, repeat to cook remaining bread.
9. Serve piping hot as is or allow to cool slightly and add toppings to create your own Native American tacos.

Cinnamon Sugar Donut Holes

Servings: 12

Cooking Time: 6 Minutes

Ingredients:

- 1 cup all-purpose flour
- 6 tablespoons cane sugar, divided
- 1 teaspoon baking powder
- 3 teaspoons ground cinnamon, divided
- ¼ teaspoon salt
- 1 large egg
- 1 teaspoon vanilla extract
- 2 tablespoons melted butter

Directions:

1. Preheat the toaster oven to 370°F.

2. In a small bowl, combine the flour, 2 tablespoons of the sugar, the baking powder, 1 teaspoon of the cinnamon, and the salt. Mix well.

3. In a larger bowl, whisk together the egg, vanilla extract, and butter.

4. Slowly add the dry ingredients into the wet until all the ingredients are uniformly combined. Set the bowl inside the refrigerator for at least 30 minutes.

5. Before you're ready to cook, in a small bowl, mix together the remaining 4 tablespoons of sugar and 2 teaspoons of cinnamon.

6. Liberally spray the air fryer oven with olive oil mist so the donut holes don't stick to the bottom.

7. Remove the dough from the refrigerator and divide it into 12 equal donut holes. You can use a 1-ounce serving scoop if you have one.

8. Roll each donut hole in the sugar and cinnamon mixture; then place in the air fryer oven. Repeat until all the donut holes are covered in the sugar and cinnamon mixture.

9. When the oven is full, air-fry for 6 minutes. Remove the donut holes from the oven using oven-safe tongs and let cool 5 minutes. Repeat until all 12 are cooked.

Autumn Berry Dessert

Servings: 4

Cooking Time: 5 Minutes

Ingredients:

- ½ cup nonfat sour cream
- ½ cup nonfat plain yogurt
- 3 tablespoons brown sugar
- 1 16-ounce package frozen blueberries or
- 2 cups fresh blueberries, rinsed well and drained
- 1 16-ounce package frozen sliced strawberries or 2 cups sliced fresh strawberries
- 4 tablespoons ground walnuts or pecans
- Grated lemon zest

Directions:

1. Beat together the sour cream, yogurt, and brown sugar in a small bowl with an electric mixer until smooth. Set aside.

2. Combine the berries in an oiled or nonstick 8½ × 8½ × 2-inch square baking (cake) pan.

3. BROIL for 5 minutes, or until bubbling. Fill 4 individual 1-cup-size ovenproof dishes with equal portions of the berries and top with the yogurt/sour cream mixture. Serve immediately or reheat by broiling for 1 or 2 minutes prior to serving. Sprinkle each serving with a tablespoon of ground walnuts or a pinch of lemon zest.

Cinnamon Swirl Bread

Servings: 4

Cooking Time: 50 Minutes

Ingredients:

- 2 cups all-purpose flour
- 1 cup granulated sugar

- 1 teaspoon baking soda
- ½ teaspoon table salt
- 1 teaspoon cider vinegar
- 1 cup whole milk
- 1 large egg
- ¼ cup canola or vegetable oil
- FILLING
- ½ cup granulated sugar
- 1 tablespoon ground cinnamon
- GLAZE
- ¼ cup confectioners' sugar
- 2 teaspoons whole milk

Directions:

1. Preheat the toaster oven to 350 ºF. Grease the bottom of a 9 x 5-inch loaf pan.

2. Combine the flour, granulated sugar, baking soda, and salt in a large bowl. Place the vinegar in a 1-cup liquid measuring cup and add the milk; stir to combine. Whisk the milk mixture, egg, and oil in a medium bowl. Stir into the flour mixture, blending until combined.

3. Make the filling: Combine the granulated sugar and cinnamon in a small bowl.

4. Pour half of the batter into the prepared pan. Sprinkle half the cinnamon-sugar mixture over the batter in the loaf pan. Top with the remaining batter and sprinkle with remaining cinnamon-sugar mixture. Using a butter knife, make deep swirls in the batter. Make sure most of the cinnamon-sugar mixture from the top is covered in batter.

5. Bake for 45 to 50 minutes, or until a wooden pick inserted into the center comes out clean. Cool on a wire rack for 10 minutes. Run a knife around the edges of the bread, then remove the bread from the pan. Cool for an additional 10 minutes.

6. Meanwhile, make the glaze: Whisk the confectioners' sugar and milk in a small bowl until smooth. Drizzle the glaze over the partially cooled loaf. Serve warm or at room temperature.

Baked Grapefruit

Servings: 4
Cooking Time: 20 Minutes

Ingredients:

- 1 grapefruit, cut in half
- 2 tablespoons currant jelly
- 2 tablespoons ground almonds, walnuts, or pecans
- 2 tablespoons chopped raisins

Directions:

1. Preheat the toaster oven to 350° F.

2. Section the grapefruit halves with a serrated knife. Place them in an oiled or nonstick 8½ × 8½ × 2-inch square baking (cake) pan. Spread 1 tablespoon currant jelly on each half and sprinkle each with 1 tablespoon ground nuts and 1 tablespoon chopped raisins.

3. BAKE for 20 minutes, or until the grapefruit is lightly browned.

Baked Meringue Apples

Servings: 4
Cooking Time: 60 Minutes

Ingredients:

- Filling:
- 4 tablespoons chopped dried fruit
- 2 tablespoons chopped walnuts
- 1 tablespoon brown sugar
- 1 teaspoon ground cinnamon
- 1 tablespoon lemon juice
- 4 Granny Smith apples, peeled and cored
- ½ cup dry white wine

- Meringue:
- 2 egg whites
- 2 tablespoons granulated sugar

Directions:

1. Preheat the toaster oven to 375° F.

2. Combine the filling ingredients in a small bowl and fill the apple cavities in equal portions. Place the apples in an oiled or nonstick 8½ × 8½ × 2-inch square baking (cake) pan and pour the wine over them.

3. BAKE for 50 minutes, or until the apples are tender. Cool.

4. Beat the egg whites and sugar together in a small bowl until stiff and top the apples with the meringue.

5. BAKE at 350° F. for 10 minutes, or until the meringue is lightly browned.

Soft Pretzels

Servings: 12

Cooking Time: 6 Minutes

Ingredients:

- 2 teaspoons yeast
- 1 cup water, warm
- 1 teaspoon sugar
- 1 teaspoon salt
- 2½ cups all-purpose flour
- 2 tablespoons butter, melted
- 1 cup boiling water
- 1 tablespoon baking soda
- coarse sea salt
- melted butter

Directions:

1. Combine the yeast and water in a small bowl. Combine the sugar, salt and flour in the bowl of a stand mixer. With the mixer running and using the dough hook, drizzle in the yeast mixture and melted butter and knead dough until smooth and elastic – about 10 minutes. Shape into a ball and let the dough rise for 1 hour.

2. Punch the dough down to release any air and decide what size pretzels you want to make.

3. a. To make large pretzels, divide the dough into 12 portions.

4. b. To make medium sized pretzels, divide the dough into 24 portions.

5. c. To make mini pretzel knots, divide the dough into 48 portions.

6. Roll each portion into a skinny rope using both hands on the counter and rolling from the center to the ends of the rope. Spin the rope into a pretzel shape (or tie the rope into a knot) and place the tied pretzels on a parchment lined baking sheet.

7. Preheat the toaster oven to 350°F.

8. Combine the boiling water and baking soda in a shallow bowl and whisk to dissolve (this mixture will bubble, but it will settle down). Let the water cool so that you can put your hands in it. Working in batches, dip the pretzels (top side down) into the baking soda-water mixture and let them soak for 30 seconds to a minute. (This step is what gives pretzels their texture and helps them to brown faster.) Then, remove the pretzels carefully and return them (top side up) to the baking sheet. Sprinkle the coarse salt on the top.

9. Air-fry in batches for 3 minutes per side. When the pretzels are finished, brush them generously with the melted butter and enjoy them warm with some spicy mustard.

Baked Eggs With Bacon-tomato Sauce

Servings: 1
Cooking Time: 12 Minutes

Ingredients:

- 1 teaspoon olive oil
- 2 tablespoons finely chopped onion
- 1 teaspoon chopped fresh oregano
- pinch crushed red pepper flakes
- 1 (14-ounce) can crushed or diced tomatoes
- salt and freshly ground black pepper
- 2 slices of bacon, chopped
- 2 large eggs
- ¼ cup grated Cheddar cheese
- fresh parsley, chopped

Directions:

1. Start by making the tomato sauce. Preheat a medium saucepan over medium heat on the stovetop. Add the olive oil and sauté the onion, oregano and pepper flakes for 5 minutes. Add the tomatoes and bring to a simmer. Season with salt and freshly ground black pepper and simmer for 10 minutes.

2. Meanwhile, preheat the toaster oven to 400°F and pour a little water into the bottom of the air fryer oven. (This will help prevent the grease that drips into the bottom drawer from burning and smoking.) Place the bacon in the air fryer oven and air-fry at 400°F for 5 minutes.

3. When the bacon is almost crispy, remove it to a paper-towel lined plate and rinse out the air fryer oven, draining away the bacon grease.

4. Transfer the tomato sauce to a shallow 7-inch pie dish. Crack the eggs on top of the sauce and scatter the cooked bacon back on top. Season with salt and freshly ground black pepper and transfer the pie dish into the air fryer oven. You can use an aluminum foil sling to help with this by taking a long piece of aluminum foil, folding it in half lengthwise twice until it is roughly 26-inches by 3-inches. Place this under the pie dish and hold the ends of the foil to move the pie dish in and out of the air fryer oven. Tuck the ends of the foil beside the pie dish while it cooks in the air fryer oven.

5. Air-fry at 400°F for 5 minutes, or until the eggs are almost cooked to your liking. Sprinkle cheese on top and air-fry for an additional 2 minutes. When the cheese has melted, remove the pie dish from the air fryer oven, sprinkle with a little chopped parsley and let the eggs cool for a few minutes – just enough time to toast some buttered bread in your air fryer oven!

Apple Incredibles

Servings: 6
Cooking Time: 25 Minutes

Ingredients:

- Muffin mixture:
- 2 cups unbleached flour
- 1 teaspoon baking powder
- ¼ cup brown sugar
- ½ teaspoon salt
- ¼ cup margarine, at room temperature
- ½ cup skim milk
- 1 egg, beaten
- 2 tablespoons finely chopped raisins
- 2 tablespoons finely chopped pecans
- 1 apple, peeled, cored, and thinly sliced

Directions:

1. Preheat the toaster oven to 400° F.

2. Combine the muffin mixture ingredients in a large bowl, stirring just to blend. Fill the pans of

an oiled or nonstick 6-muffin tin with the batter. Insert the apple slices vertically into the batter, standing and pushing them all the way down to the bottom of the pan.

3. BAKE for 25 minutes, or until the apples are tender and the muffins are lightly browned.

Portobello Burgers

Servings: 4
Cooking Time: 12 Minutes

Ingredients:
- 4 multigrain hamburger buns Dijon mustard
- 4 large portobello mushroom caps, stemmed and brushed clean
- 2 tablespoons olive oil
- Garlic powder
- Salt and butcher's pepper
- 4 thin onion slices
- 4 tomato slices

Directions:
1. TOAST the split hamburger buns and spread each slice with mustard. Set aside.
2. Brush both sides of the mushroom caps with olive oil and sprinkle with garlic powder and salt and pepper to taste.
3. BROIL the caps on a broiling rack with a pan underneath, ribbed side up, for 6 minutes. Turn the mushrooms carefully with tongs and broil again for 6 minutes, or until lightly browned. Place the mushroom caps on the bottom buns and layer each with an onion and tomato slice. Top with the remaining bun halves and serve.

Good Stuff Bread

Servings: 2
Cooking Time: 40 Minutes

Ingredients:

- First mixture:
- 1 apple, peeled and grated
- 1 carrot, peeled and grated
- 1 cup unbleached flour
- 2 teaspoons baking powder
- ⅓ cup chopped walnuts
- ⅓ cup raisins
- ⅓ cup rolled oats
- ⅓ cup shredded sweetened coconut
- Blending mixture:
- 1 banana
- 1 egg
- 1 cup low-fat buttermilk
- 2 tablespoons dark brown sugar
- 2 tablespoons vegetable oil
- Salt to taste

Directions:
1. Preheat the toaster oven to 375° F.
2. Combine all the first mixture ingredients in a medium bowl and stir to mix well. Set aside.
3. Process all the blending mixture ingredients in a blender or food processor until the mixture is smooth. Add to the first mixture ingredients and stir to mix thoroughly. Transfer to an oiled or nonstick 8½ × 4½ × 2¼-inch regular size loaf pan.
4. BAKE for 40 minutes, or until a toothpick inserted in the center comes out clean and the top is well browned.

Cinnamon Biscuit Rolls

Servings: 12
Cooking Time: 5 Minutes

Ingredients:
- Dough
- ¼ cup warm water (105–115°F)
- 1 teaspoon active dry yeast
- 1 tablespoon sugar

- ½ cup buttermilk, lukewarm
- 2 cups flour, plus more for dusting
- 1 teaspoon baking powder
- ½ teaspoon salt
- 3 tablespoons cold butter
- Filling
- 1 tablespoon butter, melted
- 1 teaspoon cinnamon
- 2 tablespoons sugar
- Icing
- ⅔ cup powdered sugar
- ¼ teaspoon vanilla
- 2–3 teaspoons milk

Directions:

1. Dissolve yeast and sugar in warm water. Add buttermilk, stir, and set aside.

2. In a large bowl, sift together flour, baking powder, and salt. Using knives or a pastry blender, cut in butter until mixture is well combined and crumbly.

3. Pour in buttermilk mixture and stir with fork until a ball of dough forms.

4. Knead dough on a lightly floured surface for 5 minutes. Roll into an 8 x 11-inch rectangle.

5. For the filling, spread the melted butter over the dough.

6. In a small bowl, stir together the cinnamon and sugar, then sprinkle over dough.

7. Starting on a long side, roll up dough so that you have a roll about 11 inches long. Cut into 12 slices with a serrated knife and sawing motion so slices remain round.

8. Place rolls on a plate or cookie sheet about an inch apart and let rise for 30 minutes.

9. For icing, mix the powdered sugar, vanilla, and milk. Stir and add additional milk until icing reaches a good spreading consistency.

10. Preheat the toaster oven to 360°F.

11. Place 6 cinnamon rolls in baking pan and cook 5 minutes or until top springs back when lightly touched. Repeat to cook remaining 6 rolls.

12. Spread icing over warm rolls and serve.

FISH AND SEAFOOD

Snapper With Capers And Olives

Servings: 2
Cooking Time: 10 Minutes

Ingredients:

- 2 tablespoons capers
- ¼ cup pitted and sliced black olives
- 2 tablespoons olive oil
- ½ teaspoon dried oregano
- Salt and freshly ground black pepper to taste
- 2 6-ounce red snapper fillets
- 1 tomato, cut into wedges

Directions:

1. Combine the capers, olives, olive oil, and seasonings in a bowl.

2. Place the fillets in an oiled or nonstick 8½ × 8½ × 2-inch square baking (cake) pan and spoon the caper mixture over them.

3. BROIL for 10 minutes, or until the fish flakes easily with a fork. Serve with the tomato wedges.

Ginger Miso Calamari

Servings: 4
Cooking Time: 10 Minutes

Ingredients:

- 15 ounces calamari, cleaned
- Sauce:
- 2 tablespoons dry white wine
- 2 tablespoons white miso
- 1 tablespoon balsamic vinegar
- 1 teaspoon honey
- 1 teaspoon toasted sesame oil
- 1 teaspoon olive oil
- 1 tablespoon grated fresh ginger
- Salt and white pepper to taste

Directions:

1. Slice the calamari bodies into ½-inch rings, leaving the tentacles uncut. Set aside.

2. Whisk together the sauce ingredients in a bowl. Transfer the mixture to a baking pan and add the calamari, mixing well to coat.

3. BROIL for 20 minutes, turning with tongs every 5 minutes, or until cooked but not rubbery. Serve with the sauce.

Beer-breaded Halibut Fish Tacos

Servings: 4
Cooking Time: 10 Minutes

Ingredients:

- 1 pound halibut, cut into 1-inch strips
- 1 cup light beer
- 1 jalapeño, minced and divided
- 1 clove garlic, minced
- ¼ teaspoon ground cumin
- ½ cup cornmeal
- ¼ cup all-purpose flour
- 1¼ teaspoons sea salt, divided
- 2 cups shredded cabbage
- 1 lime, juiced and divided
- ¼ cup Greek yogurt
- ¼ cup mayonnaise
- 1 cup grape tomatoes, quartered
- ½ cup chopped cilantro
- ¼ cup chopped onion
- 1 egg, whisked
- 8 corn tortillas

Directions:

1. In a shallow baking dish, place the fish, the beer, 1 teaspoon of the minced jalapeño, the

garlic, and the cumin. Cover and refrigerate for 30 minutes.

2. Meanwhile, in a medium bowl, mix together the cornmeal, flour, and ½ teaspoon of the salt.

3. In large bowl, mix together the shredded cabbage, 1 tablespoon of the lime juice, the Greek yogurt, the mayonnaise, and ½ teaspoon of the salt.

4. In a small bowl, make the pico de gallo by mixing together the tomatoes, cilantro, onion, ¼ teaspoon of the salt, the remaining jalapeño, and the remaining lime juice.

5. Remove the fish from the refrigerator and discard the marinade. Dredge the fish in the whisked egg; then dredge the fish in the cornmeal flour mixture, until all pieces of fish have been breaded.

6. Preheat the toaster oven to 350°F.

7. Place the fish in the air fryer oven and spray liberally with cooking spray. Air-fry for 6 minutes, flip the fish, and cook another 4 minutes.

8. While the fish is cooking, heat the tortillas in a heavy skillet for 1 to 2 minutes over high heat.

9. To assemble the tacos, place the battered fish on the heated tortillas, and top with slaw and pico de gallo. Serve immediately.

Light Trout Amandine

Servings: 4

Cooking Time: 15 Minutes

Ingredients:
- 1 tablespoon margarine
- ½ cup sliced almonds
- 1 tablespoon lemon juice
- 1 teaspoon Worcestershire sauce
- Salt and freshly ground black pepper
- 4 6-ounce trout fillets

- 2 tablespoons chopped fresh parsley

Directions:

1. Combine the margarine and almonds in an oiled or nonstick 8½ × 8½ × 2-inch square baking (cake) pan.

2. BROIL for 5 minutes, or until the margarine is melted. Remove the pan from the oven and add the lemon juice and Worcestershire sauce. Season to taste with salt and pepper, and stir again to blend well. Add the trout fillets and spoon the mixture over them to coat well.

3. BROIL for 10 minutes, or until the almonds and fillets are lightly browned. Garnish with the chopped parsley before serving.

Shrimp Patties

Servings: 4

Cooking Time: 10 Minutes

Ingredients:
- ½ pound shelled and deveined raw shrimp
- ¼ cup chopped red bell pepper
- ¼ cup chopped green onion
- ¼ cup chopped celery
- 2 cups cooked sushi rice
- ½ teaspoon garlic powder
- ½ teaspoon Old Bay Seasoning
- ½ teaspoon salt
- 2 teaspoons Worcestershire sauce
- ½ cup plain breadcrumbs
- oil for misting or cooking spray

Directions:

1. Finely chop the shrimp. You can do this in a food processor, but it takes only a few pulses. Be careful not to overprocess into mush.

2. Place shrimp in a large bowl and add all other ingredients except the breadcrumbs and oil. Stir until well combined.

3. Preheat the toaster oven to 390°F.

4. Shape shrimp mixture into 8 patties, no more than ½-inch thick. Roll patties in breadcrumbs and mist with oil or cooking spray.

5. Place 4 shrimp patties in air fryer oven and air-fry at 390°F for 10 minutes, until shrimp cooks through and outside is crispy.

6. Repeat step 5 to cook remaining shrimp patties.

Lemon-dill Salmon Burgers

Servings: 4

Cooking Time: 8 Minutes

Ingredients:

• 2 (6-ounce) fillets of salmon, finely chopped by hand or in a food processor
• 1 cup fine breadcrumbs
• 1 teaspoon freshly grated lemon zest
• 2 tablespoons chopped fresh dill weed
• 1 teaspoon salt
• freshly ground black pepper
• 2 eggs, lightly beaten
• 4 brioche or hamburger buns
• lettuce, tomato, red onion, avocado, mayonnaise or mustard, to serve

Directions:

1. Preheat the toaster oven to 400°F.

2. Combine all the ingredients in a bowl. Mix together well and divide into four balls. Flatten the balls into patties, making an indentation in the center of each patty with your thumb (this will help the burger stay flat as it cooks) and flattening the sides of the burgers so that they fit nicely into the air fryer oven.

3. Transfer the burgers to the air fryer oven and air-fry for 4 minutes. Flip the burgers over and

air-fry for another 3 to 4 minutes, until nicely browned and firm to the touch.

4. Serve on soft brioche buns with your choice of topping – lettuce, tomato, red onion, avocado, mayonnaise or mustard.

Almond Crab Cakes

Servings: 4

Cooking Time: 10 Minutes

Ingredients:

• 1 pound cooked lump crabmeat, drained and picked over
• ¼ cup ground almonds
• 1 tablespoon Dijon mustard
• 1 scallion, white and green parts, finely chopped
• ½ red bell pepper, finely chopped
• 1 large egg
• 1 teaspoon lemon zest
• Oil spray (hand-pumped)
• 3 tablespoons almond flour

Directions:

1. Preheat the toaster oven to 375°F on AIR FRY for 5 minutes.

2. In a medium bowl, mix the crab meat, almonds, mustard, scallion, bell pepper, egg, and lemon zest until well combined and the mixture holds together when pressed. If the crab cakes do not stick together, add more ground almond.

3. Divide the crab mixture into 8 patties and press them to about 1 inch thick. Place them on a plate, cover, and chill for 30 minutes.

4. Place the air-fryer basket in the baking tray and generously spray with the oil.

5. Place the almond flour on a plate and dredge the crab cakes until they are lightly coated.

6. Place them in the basket and lightly spray both sides with the oil.

7. In position 2, air fry for 10 minutes, turning halfway through, until golden brown. Serve.

Oven-crisped Fish Fillets With Salsa

Servings: 4

Cooking Time: 14 Minutes

Ingredients:

* Coating ingredients:
* 1 cup cornmeal
* 1 teaspoon garlic powder
* 1 teaspoon ground cumin
* 1 teaspoon paprika
* Salt to taste
* 4 6-ounce fish fillets, approximately
* ¼ to ½ inch thick
* 2 tablespoons vegetable oil

Directions:

1. Combine the coating ingredients in a small bowl, blending well. Transfer to a large plate, spreading evenly over the surface. Brush the fillets with vegetable oil and press both sides of each fillet into the coating.

2. BROIL an oiled or nonstick 8½ × 8½ × 2-inch square baking (cake) pan for 1 or 2 minutes to preheat. Remove the pan and place the fillets in the hot pan, laying them flat.

3. BROIL for 7 minutes, then remove the pan from the oven and carefully turn the fillets with a spatula. Broil for another 7 minutes, or until the fish flakes easily with a fork and the coating is crisped to your preference. Serve immediately.

Sea Scallops

Servings: 4

Cooking Time: 8 Minutes

Ingredients:

* 1½ pounds sea scallops
* salt and pepper
* 2 eggs
* ½ cup flour
* ½ cup plain breadcrumbs
* oil for misting or cooking spray

Directions:

1. Rinse scallops and remove the tough side muscle. Sprinkle to taste with salt and pepper.

2. Beat eggs together in a shallow dish. Place flour in a second shallow dish and breadcrumbs in a third.

3. Preheat the toaster oven to 390°F.

4. Dip scallops in flour, then eggs, and then roll in breadcrumbs. Mist with oil or cooking spray.

5. Place scallops in air fryer oven in a single layer, leaving some space between. You should be able to cook about a dozen at a time.

6. Air-fry at 390°F for 8 minutes, watching carefully so as not to overcook. Scallops are done when they turn opaque all the way through. They will feel slightly firm when pressed with tines of a fork.

7. Repeat step 6 to cook remaining scallops.

Bacon-wrapped Scallops

Servings: 4

Cooking Time: 8 Minutes

Ingredients:

* 16 large scallops
* 8 bacon strips
* ½ teaspoon black pepper
* ¼ teaspoon smoked paprika

Directions:

1. Pat the scallops dry with a paper towel. Slice each of the bacon strips in half. Wrap 1 bacon strip around 1 scallop and secure with a toothpick. Repeat with the remaining scallops. Season the scallops with pepper and paprika.

2. Preheat the toaster oven to 350°F.

3. Place the bacon-wrapped scallops in the air fryer oven and air-fry for 4 minutes. Cook another 6 to 7 minutes. When the bacon is crispy, the scallops should be cooked through and slightly firm, but not rubbery. Serve immediately.

Sweet Chili Shrimp

Servings: 4

Cooking Time: 6 Minutes

Ingredients:
- 1 pound jumbo shrimp, peeled and deveined
- ¼ cup sweet chili sauce
- 1 lime, zested and juiced
- 1 tablespoon soy sauce
- 1 tablespoon honey
- 1 tablespoon olive oil
- 1 large garlic clove, minced
- ½ teaspoon salt
- ¼ teaspoon pepper
- 1 green onion, thinly sliced, for garnish

Directions:
1. Place the shrimp in a large bowl. Whisk all the remaining ingredients except the green onion in a separate bowl.

2. Pour sauce over the shrimp and toss to coat.

3. Preheat the toaster Oven to 430°F.

4. Line the food tray with foil, place shrimp on the tray, then insert at top position in the preheated oven.

5. Select the Air Fry function, adjust time to 6 minutes, and press Start/Pause.

6. Remove shrimp and garnish with sliced green onions.

Crispy Calamari

Servings: 4

Cooking Time: 30 Minutes

Ingredients:
- Oil spray (hand-pumped)
- ¾ cup buttermilk
- 1 large egg
- 1 cup panko bread crumbs
- ¾ cup all-purpose flour
- ½ teaspoon sea salt or Old Bay seasoning
- 1 pound frozen squid rings, thawed and drained well or fresh
- 1 lemon, cut into wedges

Directions:
1. Preheat the toaster oven to 400°F on AIR FRY for 5 minutes.

2. Place the air-fryer basket in the baking tray and generously spray it with the oil.

3. In a medium bowl, whisk the buttermilk and egg.

4. In another medium bowl, stir the bread crumbs, flour, and salt until well blended.

5. Dredge the squid in the buttermilk mixture and then dredge it in the bread crumb mixture.

6. Place the breaded calamari in the basket in a single layer and lightly spray it with the oil. You will have to do several batches.

7. In position 2, air fry for 10 minutes until crispy and golden brown. Cover the cooked calamari with foil to keep it warm while you cook the remaining batches.

8. Repeat with the remaining calamari rings.

9. Serve with lemon wedges.

Roasted Garlic Shrimp

Servings: 4
Cooking Time: 12 Minutes

Ingredients:

- Nonstick cooking spray
- ¼ cup unsalted butter, melted
- 2 cloves garlic, minced
- 1 teaspoon grated lemon zest
- ½ teaspoon dried thyme leaves
- ¼ teaspoon freshly ground black pepper
- Kosher salt
- 1 pound uncooked large shrimp, fresh or frozen and thawed, peeled and deveined
- 1 ½ tablespoons fresh lemon juice
- Optional: Minced fresh flat-leaf (Italian) parsley

Directions:

1. Preheat the toaster oven to 400°F. Spray a 12 x 12-inch baking pan with nonstick cooking spray.
2. Mix the melted butter, garlic, lemon zest, thyme, and pepper in a small bowl. Season with salt. Set aside.
3. Arrange the shrimp in a single layer in the prepared pan. Pour the butter mixture over the shrimp, then stir gently to coat the shrimp.
4. Roast, uncovered, for 10 to 12 minutes or until the shrimp turn pink. Drizzle with the lemon juice. Transfer to a serving platter and spoon any collected drippings over the shrimp. Garnish, if desired, with minced parsley.

Fried Shrimp

Servings: 3
Cooking Time: 7 Minutes

Ingredients:

- 1 Large egg white
- 2 tablespoons Water
- 1 cup Plain dried bread crumbs (gluten-free, if a concern)
- ¼ cup All-purpose flour or almond flour
- ¼ cup Yellow cornmeal
- 1 teaspoon Celery salt
- 1 teaspoon Mild paprika
- Up to ½ teaspoon Cayenne (optional)
- ¾ pound Large shrimp (20–25 per pound), peeled and deveined
- Vegetable oil spray

Directions:

1. Preheat the toaster oven to 400°F.
2. Set two medium or large bowls on your counter. In the first, whisk the egg white and water until foamy. In the second, stir the bread crumbs, flour, cornmeal, celery salt, paprika, and cayenne (if using) until well combined.
3. Pour all the shrimp into the egg white mixture and stir gently until all the shrimp are coated. Use kitchen tongs to pick them up one by one and transfer them to the bread-crumb mixture. Turn each in the bread-crumb mixture to coat it evenly and thoroughly on all sides before setting it on a cutting board. When you're done coating the shrimp, coat them all on both sides with the vegetable oil spray.
4. Set the shrimp in as close to one layer in the air fryer oven as you can. Some may overlap. Air-fry for 7 minutes, gently rearranging the shrimp at the 4-minute mark to get covered surfaces exposed, until golden brown and firm but not hard.
5. Use kitchen tongs to gently transfer the shrimp to a wire rack. Cool for only a minute or two before serving.

Tex-mex Fish Tacos

Servings: 3
Cooking Time: 7 Minutes

Ingredients:

- ¾ teaspoon Chile powder
- ¼ teaspoon Ground cumin
- ¼ teaspoon Dried oregano
- 3 5-ounce skinless mahi-mahi fillets
- Vegetable oil spray
- 3 Corn or flour tortillas
- 6 tablespoons Diced tomatoes
- 3 tablespoons Regular, low-fat, or fat-free sour cream

Directions:

1. Preheat the toaster oven to 400°F.
2. Stir the chile powder, cumin, and oregano in a small bowl until well combined.
3. Coat each piece of fish all over (even the sides and ends) with vegetable oil spray. Sprinkle the spice mixture evenly over all sides of the fillets. Lightly spray them again.
4. When the machine is at temperature, set the fillets in the air fryer oven with as much air space between them as possible. Air-fry undisturbed for 7 minutes, until lightly browned and firm but not hard.
5. Use a nonstick-safe spatula to transfer the fillets to a wire rack. Microwave the tortillas on high for a few seconds, until supple. Put a fillet in each tortilla and top each with 2 tablespoons diced tomatoes and 1 tablespoon sour cream.

Crab-stuffed Peppers

Servings: 4
Cooking Time: 45 Minutes

Ingredients:

- Filling:
- 1½ cups fresh crabmeat, chopped, or 2 6-ounce cans lump crabmeat, drained
- 4 plum tomatoes, chopped
- 2 4-ounce cans sliced mushrooms, drained well
- 4 tablespoons pitted and sliced black olives
- 2 tablespoons olive oil
- 2 garlic cloves, minced
- ½ teaspoon ground cumin
- Salt and freshly ground black pepper to taste
- 4 large bell peppers, tops cut off, seeds and membrane removed
- ½ cup shredded low-fat mozzarella cheese

Directions:

1. Preheat the toaster oven to 375° F.
2. Combine the filling ingredients in a bowl and adjust the seasonings. Spoon the mixture to generously fill each pepper. Place the peppers upright in an 8½ × 8½ × 2-inch oiled or nonstick square (cake) pan.
3. BAKE for 40 minutes, or until the peppers are tender. Remove from the oven and sprinkle the cheese in equal portions on top of the peppers.
4. BROIL 5 minutes, or until the cheese is melted.

Skewered Salsa Verde Shrimp

Servings: 4
Cooking Time: 8 Minutes

Ingredients:

- 1½ pounds large fresh shrimp, peeled and deveined
- Brushing mixture:
- 1 7-ounce can salsa verde
- 1 teaspoon ground cumin
- ½ teaspoon chopped fresh cilantro or parsley

- 1 teaspoon garlic powder
- 3 tablespoons plain yogurt
- 1 tablespoon olive oil
- Lemon wedges

Directions:

1. Thread the shrimp onto the skewers.

2. Combine the brushing mixture ingredients in a small bowl. Adjust the seasonings and brush the shrimp with the mixture.

3. BROIL the shrimp for 4 minutes. Turn the skewers, brush the shrimp again, and broil for another 4 minutes, or until the shrimp are firm and cooked. Remove the shrimp from the skewers and serve with lemon wedges.

Catfish Kebabs

Servings: 4
Cooking Time: 20 Minutes

Ingredients:

- Marinade:
- 3 tablespoons lemon juice
- 3 tablespoons tomato juice
- 2 garlic cloves, minced
- 2 tablespoons olive oil
- 1 teaspoon soy sauce
- 4 5-ounce catfish fillets
- 4 9-inch metal skewers
- 2 plum tomatoes, quartered
- 1 onion, cut into 1 × 1-inch pieces

Directions:

1. Combine the marinade ingredients in a small bowl. Set aside.

2. Cut the fillets into 2 by 3-inch strips and place in a shallow glass or ceramic dish. Add the marinade and refrigerate, covered, for at least 20 minutes. Remove the strips from the marinade,

roll, and skewer, alternating the rolled strips with the tomatoes and onion.

3. Brush the kebabs with marinade, reserving the remaining marinade for brushing again later. Place the skewers on a broiling rack with a pan underneath.

4. Broil for 10 minutes, then remove the pan from the oven and carefully turn the skewers. Brush the kebabs with the marinade and broil again for 10 minutes, or until browned.

Crunchy And Buttery Cod With Ritz® Cracker Crust

Servings: 2
Cooking Time: 10 Minutes

Ingredients:

- 4 tablespoons butter, melted
- 8 to 10 RITZ® crackers, crushed into crumbs
- 2 (6-ounce) cod fillets
- salt and freshly ground black pepper
- 1 lemon

Directions:

1. Preheat the toaster oven to 380°F.

2. Melt the butter in a small saucepan on the stovetop or in a microwavable dish in the microwave, and then transfer the butter to a shallow dish. Place the crushed RITZ® crackers into a second shallow dish.

3. Season the fish fillets with salt and freshly ground black pepper. Dip them into the butter and then coat both sides with the RITZ® crackers.

4. Place the fish into the air fryer oven and air-fry at 380°F for 10 minutes, flipping the fish over halfway through the cooking time.

5. Serve with a wedge of lemon to squeeze over the top.

Blackened Catfish

Servings: 4
Cooking Time: 8 Minutes

Ingredients:

- 1 teaspoon paprika
- 1 teaspoon garlic powder
- 1 teaspoon onion powder
- 1 teaspoon ground dried thyme
- ½ teaspoon ground black pepper
- ⅛ teaspoon cayenne pepper
- ½ teaspoon dried oregano
- ⅛ teaspoon crushed red pepper flakes
- 1 pound catfish filets
- ½ teaspoon sea salt
- 2 tablespoons butter, melted
- 1 tablespoon extra-virgin olive oil
- 2 tablespoons chopped parsley
- 1 lemon, cut into wedges

Directions:

1. In a small bowl, stir together the paprika, garlic powder, onion powder, thyme, black pepper, cayenne pepper, oregano, and crushed red pepper flakes.
2. Pat the fish dry with paper towels. Season the filets with sea salt and then coat with the blackening seasoning.
3. In a small bowl, mix together the butter and olive oil and drizzle over the fish filets, flipping them to coat them fully.
4. Preheat the toaster oven to 350°F.
5. Place the fish in the air fryer oven and air-fry for 8 minutes, checking the fish for doneness after 4 minutes. The fish will flake easily when cooked.
6. Remove the fish from the air fryer oven. Top with chopped parsley and serve with lemon wedges.

Sesame-crusted Tuna Steaks

Servings: 3
Cooking Time: 13 Minutes

Ingredients:

- ½ cup Sesame seeds, preferably a blend of white and black
- 1½ tablespoons Toasted sesame oil
- 3 6-ounce skinless tuna steaks

Directions:

1. Preheat the toaster oven to 400°F.
2. Pour the sesame seeds on a dinner plate. Use ½ tablespoon of the sesame oil as a rub on both sides and the edges of a tuna steak. Set it in the sesame seeds, then turn it several times, pressing gently, to create an even coating of the seeds, including around the steak's edge. Set aside and continue coating the remaining steak(s).
3. When the machine is at temperature, set the steaks in the air fryer oven with as much air space between them as possible. Air-fry undisturbed for 10 minutes for medium-rare (not USDA-approved), or 12 to 13 minutes for cooked through (USDA-approved).
4. Use a nonstick-safe spatula to transfer the steaks to serving plates. Serve hot.

Horseradish-crusted Salmon Fillets

Servings: 3
Cooking Time: 8 Minutes

Ingredients:

- ½ cup Fresh bread crumbs
- 4 tablespoons (¼ cup/½ stick) Butter, melted and cooled
- ¼ cup Jarred prepared white horseradish
- Vegetable oil spray

- 4 6-ounce skin-on salmon fillets

Directions:

1. Preheat the toaster oven to 400°F.

2. Mix the bread crumbs, butter, and horseradish in a bowl until well combined.

3. Take the pan out of the machine. Generously spray the skin side of each fillet. Pick them up one by one with a nonstick-safe spatula and set them in the pan skin side down with as much air space between them as possible. Divide the bread-crumb mixture between the fillets, coating the top of each fillet with an even layer. Generously coat the bread-crumb mixture with vegetable oil spray.

4. Return the pan to the machine and air-fry undisturbed for 8 minutes, or until the topping has lightly browned and the fish is firm but not hard.

5. Use a nonstick-safe spatula to transfer the salmon fillets to serving plates. Cool for 5 minutes before serving. Because of the butter in the topping, it will stay very hot for quite a while. Take care, especially if you're serving these fillets to children.

Maple Balsamic Glazed Salmon

Servings: 4

Cooking Time: 10 Minutes

Ingredients:

- 4 (6-ounce) fillets of salmon
- salt and freshly ground black pepper
- vegetable oil
- ¼ cup pure maple syrup
- 3 tablespoons balsamic vinegar
- 1 teaspoon Dijon mustard

Directions:

1. Preheat the toaster oven to 400°F.

2. Season the salmon well with salt and freshly ground black pepper. Spray or brush the bottom of the air fryer oven with vegetable oil and place the salmon fillets inside. Air-fry the salmon for 5 minutes.

3. While the salmon is air-frying, combine the maple syrup, balsamic vinegar and Dijon mustard in a small saucepan over medium heat and stir to blend well. Let the mixture simmer while the fish is cooking. It should start to thicken slightly, but keep your eye on it so it doesn't burn.

4. Brush the glaze on the salmon fillets and air-fry for an additional 5 minutes. The salmon should feel firm to the touch when finished and the glaze should be nicely browned on top. Brush a little more glaze on top before removing and serving with rice and vegetables, or a nice green salad.

Rolled Asparagus Flounder

Servings: 4

Cooking Time: 30 Minutes

Ingredients:

- 1 dozen asparagus stalks, tough stem part cut off
- 4 6-ounce flounder fillets
- 4 tablespoons chopped scallions
- 4 tablespoons shredded carrots
- 4 tablespoons finely chopped
- Almonds
- 1 teaspoon dried dill weed
- Salt and freshly ground black pepper
- 1 lemon, cut into wedges

Directions:

1. Preheat the toaster oven to 400° F.

2. Place 3 asparagus stalks lengthwise on a flounder fillet. Add 1 tablespoon scallions, 1

tablespoon carrots, 1 tablespoon almonds, and a sprinkling of dill. Season to taste with salt and pepper and roll the fillet together so that the long edges overlap. Secure the edges with toothpicks or tie with cotton string. Carefully place the rolled fillet in an oiled or nonstick 8½ × 8½ × 2-inch square baking (cake) pan. Repeat the process for the remaining ingredients. Cover the pan with aluminum foil.

3. BAKE, covered, for 20 minutes, or until the asparagus is tender. Remove the cover.

4. BROIL, uncovered, for 10 minutes, or until the fish is lightly browned. Remove and discard the toothpicks or string. Serve the rolled filets with lemon wedges.

Shrimp & Grits

Servings: 4
Cooking Time: 5 Minutes

Ingredients:

- 1 pound raw shelled shrimp, deveined (26–30 count or smaller)
- Marinade
- 2 tablespoons lemon juice
- 2 tablespoons Worcestershire sauce
- 1 tablespoon olive oil
- 1 teaspoon Old Bay Seasoning
- ½ teaspoon hot sauce
- Grits
- ¾ cup quick cooking grits (not instant)
- 3 cups water
- ½ teaspoon salt
- 1 tablespoon butter
- ½ cup chopped green bell pepper
- ½ cup chopped celery
- ½ cup chopped onion
- ½ teaspoon oregano
- ¼ teaspoon Old Bay Seasoning
- 2 ounces sharp Cheddar cheese, grated

Directions:

1. Stir together all marinade ingredients. Pour marinade over shrimp and set aside.

2. For grits, heat water and salt to boil in saucepan on stovetop. Stir in grits, lower heat to medium-low, and cook about 5 minutes or until thick and done.

3. Place butter, bell pepper, celery, and onion in air fryer oven baking pan. Air-fry at 390°F for 2 minutes and stir. Cook 6 or 7 minutes longer, until crisp tender.

4. Add oregano and 1 teaspoon Old Bay to cooked vegetables. Stir in grits and cheese and air-fry at 390°F for 1 minute. Stir and cook 1 to 2 minutes longer to melt cheese.

5. Remove baking pan from air fryer oven. Cover with plate to keep warm while shrimp cooks.

6. Drain marinade from shrimp. Place shrimp in air fryer oven and air-fry at 360°F for 3 minutes. Cook 2 more minutes, until done.

7. To serve, spoon grits onto plates and top with shrimp.

Marinated Catfish

Servings: 4
Cooking Time: 10 Minutes

Ingredients:

- Marinade:
- 1 tablespoon olive oil
- 1 tablespoon lemon juice
- ¼ dry white wine
- 1 tablespoon garlic powder
- 1 tablespoon soy sauce
- 4 6-ounce catfish fillets

Directions:

1. Combine the marinade ingredients in an 8½ × 8½ × 4-inch ovenproof baking dish. Add the fillets and let stand for 10 minutes, spooning the marinade over the fillets every 2 minutes.

2. BROIL the fillets for 15 minutes, or until the fish flakes casily with a fork.

Broiled Lemon Coconut Shrimp

Servings: 4

Cooking Time: 10 Minutes

Ingredients:

*   Brushing mixture:
*   2 tablespoons lemon juice
*   4 tablespoons olive oil
*   1 tablespoon grated lemon zest
*   Salt to taste
*   1 pound fresh shrimp, peeled, deveined, and butterflied
*   ½ cup grated unsweetened coconut

Directions:

1. Combine the brushing mixture ingredients in a small bowl. Add the shrimp and toss to coat well. Set aside.

2. Place the coconut on a plate, spreading it out evenly.

3. Press each shrimp into the coconut, coating well on all sides. Place the shrimp in an 8½ × 8½ × 2-inch oiled or nonstick square (cake) pan.

4. BROIL the shrimp for 5 minutes, turn with tongs, and broil for 5 more minutes, or until browned lightly.

Fish And "chips"

Servings: 2

Cooking Time: 10 Minutes

Ingredients:

*   ½ cup flour
*   ½ teaspoon paprika
*   ¼ teaspoon ground white pepper (or freshly ground black pepper)
*   1 egg
*   ¼ cup mayonnaise
*   2 cups salt & vinegar kettle cooked potato chips, coarsely crushed
*   12 ounces cod
*   tartar sauce
*   lemon wedges

Directions:

1. Set up a dredging station. Combine the flour, paprika and pepper in a shallow dish. Combine the egg and mayonnaise in a second shallow dish. Place the crushed potato chips in a third shallow dish.

2. Cut the cod into 6 pieces. Dredge each piece of fish in the flour, then dip it into the egg mixture and then place it into the crushed potato chips. Make sure all sides of the fish are covered and pat the chips gently onto the fish so they stick well.

3. Preheat the toaster oven to 370°F.

4. Place the coated fish fillets into the air fry oven. (It is ok if a couple of pieces slightly overlap or rest on top of other fillets in order to fit everything in the air fryer oven.)

5. Air-fry for 10 minutes, gently turning the fish over halfway through the cooking time.

6. Transfer the fish to a platter and serve with tartar sauce and lemon wedges.

LUNCH AND DINNER

Chicken Marengo

Servings: 4
Cooking Time: 30 Minutes

Ingredients:

- Chicken mixture:
- 2 skinless, boneless chicken breast halves, cut into 1 × 1-inch pieces
- 6 large shrimp, peeled, deveined, and cut into 1 × 1-inch pieces
- 2 plum tomatoes, chopped
- 1 tablespoon olive oil
- ½ cup dry white wine
- 3 garlic cloves, chopped
- 6 fresh mushrooms, rinsed quickly, patted dry, and thinly sliced
- 1 teaspoon dried tarragon
- 1 tablespoon chopped fresh parsley
- Salt and freshly ground black pepper to taste
- 2 hard-boiled eggs, peeled and sliced
- ½ cup pitted and sliced black olives
- 2 tablespoons chopped fresh parsley

Directions:

1. Preheat the toaster oven to 375° F.
2. Combine the chicken mixture ingredients in a 1-quart 8½ × 8½ × 4-inch ovenproof baking dish and adjust the seasonings to taste. Cover with aluminum foil.
3. BAKE, covered, for 30 minutes, or until the chicken and shrimp are tender.
4. Garnish with slices of hard-boiled eggs, black olives, and parsley.

Classic Beef Stew

Servings: 4

Cooking Time: 50 Minutes

Ingredients:

- 1½ cups dark beer
- 4 tablespoons unbleached flour
- 2 cups (approximately 1 pound) lean top round steak, cut into 1-inch cubes
- 1 cup peeled and coarsely chopped carrots
- 1 cup peeled and coarsely chopped potatoes
- ½ cup coarsely chopped onion
- 1 cup fresh or frozen peas
- 2 plum tomatoes, chopped
- 3 garlic cloves, minced
- 4 3 bay leaves
- ¼ teaspoon ground cumin
- Salt and butcher's pepper to taste

Directions:

1. Preheat the toaster oven to 400° F.
2. Whisk together the beer and flour in a 1-quart 8½ × 8½ × 4-inch ovenproof baking dish. Add all the other ingredients and seasonings and mix well, adjusting the seasonings to taste. Cover the dish with aluminum foil.
3. BAKE, covered, for 50 minutes, or until the meat is cooked and the vegetables are tender. Remove the bay leaves before serving.

Parmesan Artichoke Pizza

Servings: 6
Cooking Time: 15 Minutes

Ingredients:

- CRUST
- ¾ cup warm water (110°F)
- 1 ½ teaspoons active dry yeast
- ¼ teaspoon sugar
- 1 tablespoon olive oil

- 1 teaspoon table salt
- ⅓ cup whole wheat flour
- 1 ½ to 1 ⅔ cups bread flour
- TOPPINGS
- 2 tablespoons olive oil
- 1 teaspoon Italian seasoning
- 1 clove garlic, minced
- ½ cup whole milk ricotta cheese, at room temperature
- ⅔ cup drained, chopped marinated artichokes
- ¼ cup chopped red onion
- 3 tablespoons minced fresh basil
- ½ cup shredded Parmesan cheese
- ⅓ cup shredded mozzarella cheese

Directions:

1. Make the Crust: Place the warm water, yeast, and sugar in a large mixing bowl for a stand mixer. Stir, then let stand for 3 to 5 minutes or until bubbly.

2. Stir in the olive oil, salt, whole wheat flour, and 1 ½ cups bread flour. If the dough is too sticky, stir in an additional 1 to 2 tablespoons bread flour. Beat with the flat (paddle) beater at medium-speed for 5 minutes (or knead by hand for 5 to 7 minutes or until the dough is smooth and elastic). Place in a greased large bowl, turn the dough over, cover with a clean towel, and let stand for 30 to 45 minutes, or until starting to rise.

3. Stir the olive oil, Italian seasoning, and garlic in a small bowl; set aside.

4. Preheat the toaster oven to 450°F. Place a 12-inch pizza pan in the toaster oven while it is preheating.

5. Turn the dough onto a lightly floured surface and pull or roll the dough to make a 12-inch circle. Carefully transfer the crust to the hot pan.

6. Brush the olive oil mixture over the crust. Spread the ricotta evenly over the crust. Top with the artichokes, red onions, fresh basil, Parmesan, and mozzarella. Bake for 13 to 15 minutes, or until the crust is golden brown and the cheese is melted. Let stand for 5 minutes before cutting.

Miso-glazed Salmon With Broccoli

Servings: 2

Cooking Time: 25 Minutes

Ingredients:

- Nonstick cooking spray
- 2 tablespoons miso, preferably yellow
- 2 tablespoons mirin
- 1 tablespoon packed dark brown sugar
- 2 teaspoons minced fresh ginger
- 1 ½ teaspoons sesame oil
- 8 ounces fresh broccoli, cut into spears
- 1 tablespoon canola or vegetable oil
- Kosher salt and freshly ground black pepper
- 2 salmon fillets (5 to 6 ounces each)

Directions:

1. Preheat the toaster oven to 425°F. Spray a 12 x 12-inch baking pan with nonstick cooking spray.

2. Stir the miso, mirin, brown sugar, ginger, and sesame oil in a small bowl; set aside.

3. Toss the broccoli spears with the canola oil and season with salt and pepper. Place the broccoli on the pan. Bake, uncovered, for 10 minutes. Stir the broccoli and move to one side of the pan.

4. Place the salmon, skin side down, on the other end of the pan. Brush lightly with olive oil and season with salt and pepper. Bake for 10 minutes.

5. Brush the fish generously with the miso sauce. Bake for an additional 3 to 5 minutes, or until the fish flakes easily with a fork and a meat thermometer registers 145°F.

Baked Tomato Casserole

Servings: 4
Cooking Time:45 Minutes

Ingredients:
- Casserole mixture:
- 1 medium onion, coarsely chopped
- 3 medium tomatoes, coarsely chopped
- 1 medium green pepper, coarsely chopped
- 2 garlic cloves, minced
- ½ teaspoon crushed oregano
- ½ teaspoon crushed basil
- 1 tablespoon extra virgin olive oil
- 2 tablespoons chopped fresh cilantro
- Salt and freshly ground black pepper
- 3 4 tablespoons grated Parmesan cheese
- ¼ cup multigrain bread crumbs

Directions:
1. Preheat the toaster oven to 400° F.
2. Combine the casserole mixture ingredients in a 1-quart 8½ × 8½ × 4-inch ovenproof baking dish. Adjust the seasonings to taste and cover with aluminum foil.
3. BAKE, covered, for 35 minutes, or until the tomatoes and pepper are tender. Remove from the oven, uncover, and sprinkle with the bread crumbs and Parmesan cheese.
4. BROIL for 10 minutes, or until the topping is lightly browned.

Parmesan Crusted Tilapia

Servings: 2
Cooking Time: 14 Minutes

Ingredients:
- 2 ounces Parmesan cheese
- 1/4 cup Italian seasoned Panko bread crumbs
- 1/2 teaspoon Italian seasoning
- 1/4 teaspoon ground black pepper
- 1 tablespoon mayonnaise
- 2 tilapia fillets or other white fish fillets (about 4 ounces each)

Directions:
1. Preheat the toaster oven to 425°F. Spray baking pan with nonstick cooking spray.
2. Using a spiralizer, grate Parmesan cheese and place in a large resealable plastic bag. Add Panko bread crumbs, Italian seasoning and black pepper. Seal and shake bag.
3. Spread mayonnaise on both sides of fish fillets. Add fish to bag and shake until coated with crumb mixture.
4. Press remaining crumbs from bag onto fish. Place on prepared baking pan.
5. Bake until fish flakes easily with a fork, 12 to 14 minutes.

Creamy Roasted Pepper Basil Soup

Servings: 4
Cooking Time: 35 Minutes

Ingredients:
- 1 5-ounce jar roasted peppers, drained ½ cup fresh basil leaves
- 1 cup fat-free half-and-half
- 1 cup skim milk
- 2 tablespoons reduced-fat cream cheese
- 1 teaspoon garlic powder
- 1 teaspoon paprika
- Salt and freshly ground black pepper to taste

- 2 tablespoons chopped fresh basil leaves (garnish for cold soup)
- 2 tablespoons grated Parmesan cheese (topping for hot soup)

Directions:

1. Preheat the toaster oven to 400° F.
2. Process all the ingredients in a blender or food processor until smooth. Transfer the mixture to a 1-quart 8½ × 8½ × 4-inch ovenproof baking dish.
3. BAKE, covered, for 35 minutes. Ladle into individual soup bowls and serve.

Salad Lentils

Servings: 4
Cooking Time: 35 Minutes

Ingredients:

- ¼ cup lentils
- 1 tablespoon olive oil
- Salad ingredients:
- 1 celery stalk, trimmed and Chopped
- 1 plum tomato, chopped
- 1 cucumber, peeled, seeded, and chopped
- 1½ cups spinach leaves, pulled into small pieces
- 1 tablespoon balsamic vinegar
- 1 tablespoon olive oil
- ½ teaspoon dried oregano
- 1 tablespoon chopped scallions
- 2 tablespoons sliced pitted black olives
- 1 teaspoon minced roasted garlic

Directions:

1. Preheat the toaster oven to 400° F.
2. Combine the lentils, ¼ cups water, and olive oil in a 1-quart 8½ × 8½ × 4-inch ovenproof baking dish. Cover with aluminum foil.
3. BAKE, covered, for 35 minutes, or until the lentils are tender. When cool, combine with all the salad ingredients in a serving bowl and toss well. Adjust the seasonings, chill, and serve.

Roasted Vegetable Gazpacho

Servings: 4
Cooking Time: 35 Minutes

Ingredients:

- Vegetables and seasonings:
- 1 bell pepper, thinly sliced
- ½ cup chopped celery
- ½ cup frozen or canned corn
- 1 medium onion, thinly sliced
- 1 small yellow squash, cut into 1-inch slices
- 1 small zucchini, cut into 1-inch slices
- 3 garlic cloves, chopped
- ½ teaspoon ground cumin
- 2 tablespoons olive oil
- Salt and freshly ground black pepper to taste
- 1 quart tomato juice
- 1 tablespoon lemon juice
- 3 tablespoons chopped fresh cilantro

Directions:

1. Preheat the toaster oven to 400°F.
2. Combine the vegetables and seasonings in an oiled or nonstick 8½ × 8½ × 2-inch square baking (cake) pan, mixing well.
3. BAKE, covered, for 25 minutes, or until the onions and celery are tender. Remove from the oven, uncover, and turn the vegetable pieces with tongs.
4. BROIL for 10 minutes, or until the vegetables are lightly browned. Remove from the oven and cool. Transfer to a large nonaluminum container and add the tomato juice, lemon juice, and cilantro. Adjust the seasonings.
5. Chill, covered, for several hours, preferably a day or two to enrich the flavor of the stock.

Healthy Southwest Stuffed Peppers

Servings: 6
Cooking Time: 30 Minutes

Ingredients:

- 1 tablespoon oil
- 1 small onion, chopped
- 1 garlic clove, minced
- 1/2 pound ground turkey
- 1/2 cup drained black beans
- 1/2 cup whole kernel corn
- 1 jar (16 oz.) medium salsa, divided
- 1/2 cup cooked white rice
- 1/2 teaspoon chili powder
- 1/2 teaspoon salt
- 1/4 teaspoon ground cumin
- 1/4 teaspoon black pepper
- 3 medium peppers, halved lengthwise leaving stem on, seeded
- 1/3 cup shredded Monterey Jack cheese, divided
- Sour cream
- Chopped fresh cilantro

Directions:

1. Preheat the toaster oven to 350°F. Spray baking pan with nonstick cooking spray.
2. In a large skillet over medium-high, heat oil. Add onion and garlic, cook for 2 to 3 minutes.
3. Add turkey to skillet, cook, stirring frequently, for 6 to 8 minutes or until turkey is cooked through.
4. Stir black beans, corn, 1/2 cup salsa, rice, chili powder, salt, cumin and pepper into turkey mixture.
5. Fill each pepper half with turkey mixture, dividing mixture evenly among peppers.
6. Top each pepper half with remaining salsa.
7. Bake 20 minutes. Sprinkle with cheese and bake an additional 10 minutes or until heated through.
8. Top with sour cream and cilantro.

Classic Tuna Casserole

Servings: 4
Cooking Time: 65 Minutes

Ingredients:

- 1 cup elbow macaroni
- 2 6-ounce cans tuna packed in water, drained well and crumbled
- 1 cup frozen peas 1 6-ounce can button mushrooms, drained
- 1 tablespoon margarine
- Salt and freshly ground black pepper
- 1 cup fat-free half-and-half
- 4 tablespoons unbleached flour
- 1 teaspoon garlic powder
- 1 cup multigrain bread crumbs

Directions:

1. Preheat the toaster oven to 400° F.
2. Combine the macaroni and 3 cups water in a 1-quart 8½ × 8½ × 4-inch ovenproof baking dish, stirring to blend well. Cover with aluminum foil.
3. BAKE, covered, for 35 minutes, or until the macaroni is tender. Remove from the oven and drain well. Return to the baking dish and add the tuna, peas, and mushrooms. Add salt and pepper to taste.
4. Whisk together the half-and-half, flour, and garlic powder in a small bowl until smooth. Add to the macaroni mixture and stir to blend well.
5. BAKE, covered, for 25 minutes. Remove from the oven, sprinkle the top with the bread crumbs, and dot with the margarine. Bake, uncovered, for 10 minutes, or until the top is browned.

Yeast Dough For Two Pizzas

Servings: 8
Cooking Time: 20 Minutes

Ingredients:

- ¼ cup tepid water
- 1 cup tepid skim milk
- ½ teaspoon sugar
- 1 1¼-ounce envelope dry yeast
- 2 cups unbleached flour
- 1 tablespoon olive oil

Directions:

1. Preheat the toaster oven to 400° F.
2. Combine the water, milk, and sugar in a bowl. Add the yeast and set aside for 3 to 5 minutes, or until the yeast is dissolved.
3. Stir in the flour gradually, adding just enough to form a ball of the dough.
4. KNEAD on a floured surface until the dough is satiny, and then put the dough in a bowl in a warm place with a damp towel over the top. In 1 hour or when the dough has doubled in bulk, punch it down and divide it in half. Flatten the dough and spread it out to the desired thickness on an oiled or nonstick 9¾-inch-diameter pie pan. Spread with Homemade Pizza Sauce (recipe follows) and add any desired toppings.
5. BAKE for 20 minutes, or until the topping ingredients are cooked and the cheese is melted.

Spicy Oven-baked Chili

Servings: 6
Cooking Time: 30 Minutes

Ingredients:

- 1 pound lean ground turkey or ground chicken breast or 1 pound lean ground sirloin or round steak
- 1 15-ounce can black beans, drained
- 1 8-ounce can tomato sauce
- ¾ cup chopped onion
- ¼ cup dry white wine
- 1 cup tomato salsa
- 1 tablespoon garlic powder
- 1 tablespoon chili powder
- 2 ⅛ teaspoon cayenne
- 3 teaspoons unsweetened cocoa
- Salt and butcher's pepper to taste

Directions:

1. Preheat the toaster oven to 375° F.
2. Combine all the ingredients in a 1-quart 8½ × 8½ × 4-inch ovenproof baking dish and mix well. Adjust the seasonings to taste. Cover with aluminum foil.
3. BAKE, covered, for 30 minutes.

Sheet Pan Loaded Nachos

Servings: 4
Cooking Time: 13 Minutes

Ingredients:

- 1 tablespoon canola or vegetable oil
- ½ pound lean ground beef
- ½ cup chopped onion
- 2 cloves garlic, minced
- 1 teaspoon chili powder
- ½ teaspoon ground cumin
- Kosher salt and freshly ground black pepper
- 6 ounces tortilla chips
- ½ cup canned black beans, rinsed and drained
- 1 ½ cups shredded sharp cheddar cheese or Mexican blend cheese
- ½ cup salsa
- Optional toppings: sliced jalapeño peppers, chopped bell peppers, sliced ripe olives, chopped

tomatoes, minced fresh cilantro, sour cream, chopped avocado, guacamole, or chopped onion.

Directions:

1. Preheat the toaster oven to 400°F. Line a 12 x 12-inch baking pan with nonstick aluminum foil. (Or if lining the pan with regular foil, spray it with nonstick cooking spray.)

2. Heat the oil in a large skillet over medium-high heat. Add the ground beef and onion and cook, stirring frequently, until the beef is almost done. Add the garlic, chili powder, cumin, season with salt and pepper, and cook, stirring frequently, until the beef is fully cooked; drain.

3. Arrange the tortilla chips in an even layer in the prepared pan. Top with the beef-onion mixture, then top with the beans. Bake, uncovered, for 6 to 8 minutes. Top with the cheese and bake for 5 minutes more, or until the cheese is melted.

4. Drizzle with the salsa. Top as desired with any of the various toppings.

Lentil And Carrot Soup

Servings: 4

Cooking Time: 40 Minutes

Ingredients:

- ½ cup lentils
- ½ cup dry white wine
- 1 small onion, chopped
- 3 carrots, peeled and finely chopped
- ½ cup fresh mushrooms, cleaned and sliced, or 1 5-ounce can mushroom pieces, well drained
- 3 garlic cloves, minced
- 1 tablespoon chopped fresh parsley
- 1 tablespoon Worcestershire sauce
- Salt and freshly ground black pepper to taste

Directions:

1. Preheat the toaster oven to 375° F.

2. Combine all the ingredients with 2 cups water in a 1-quart 8½ × 8½ × 4-inch ovenproof baking dish. Adjust the seasonings.

3. BAKE for 40 minutes, or until the lentils, carrots, and onions are tender. Ladle into individual soup bowls and serve.

Cheesy Chicken–stuffed Shells

Servings: 4

Cooking Time: 40 Minutes

Ingredients:

- Nonstick cooking spray
- 16 jumbo pasta shells
- 1 cup finely diced cooked chicken
- 1 cup whole milk ricotta cheese
- 1 ¼ cups shredded mozzarella cheese
- 1 large egg, slightly beaten
- ⅓ cup grated Parmesan cheese
- 1 teaspoon Italian seasoning
- 2 cloves garlic, minced
- ¼ teaspoon kosher salt
- ¼ teaspoon freshly ground black pepper
- 1 ½ cups marinara sauce

Directions:

1. Preheat the toaster oven to 350 ºF. Spray an 8 x 8-inch square baking pan with nonstick cooking spray.

2. Cook the shells according to the package directions, drain, and rinse with cool water.

3. Combine the chicken, ricotta, ¾ cup of the mozzarella, egg, Parmesan, Italian seasoning, garlic, salt, and pepper in a large bowl.

4. Spread about ¾ cup of the marinara sauce in the prepared pan. Fill each shell with a heaping tablespoon of the chicken-cheese mixture. Place

the prepared shells, stuffed side up, in the pan. Pour the remaining marinara over the shells.

5. Cover and bake for 25 to 30 minutes. Sprinkle with the remaining ½ cup mozzarella and bake, uncovered, for an additional 5 to 10 minutes or until the cheese is melted. Remove from the oven and let stand for 5 to 10 minutes before serving.

Lima Bean And Artichoke Casserole

Servings: 4
Cooking Time: 40 Minutes

Ingredients:
- 1 15-ounce can lima beans, drained
- 1 6-ounce jar artichokes, marinated in olive oil (include the oil)
- ½ cup dry white wine
- 1 small onion, thinly sliced
- 2 medium carrots, thinly sliced
- 1 5-ounce can roasted peppers, drained and chopped
- ¼ teaspoon paprika
- ½ teaspoon ground cumin
- 1 teaspoon curry powder
- Salt and freshly ground black pepper to taste

Directions:
1. Preheat the toaster oven to 350° F.
2. Combine all the ingredients in a 1-quart 8½ × 8½ × 4-inch ovenproof baking dish, blending well. Adjust the seasonings to taste. Cover with aluminum foil.
3. BAKE, covered, for 40 minutes, or until the carrots and onion are tender.

Gardener's Rice

Servings: 4

Cooking Time: 40 Minutes

Ingredients:
- ½ cup rice
- 2 tablespoons finely chopped scallions
- 2 small zucchini, finely chopped
- 1 bell pepper, finely chopped
- 1 small tomato, finely chopped
- ¼ cup frozen peas
- ¼ cup frozen corn
- 1 teaspoon ground cumin
- ½ teaspoon dried oregano or
- 1 teaspoon chopped fresh oregano
- Salt and freshly ground black pepper to taste

Directions:
1. Preheat the toaster oven to 400° F.
2. Combine all the ingredients with ¼ cups water in a 1-quart 8½ × 8½ × 4-inch ovenproof baking dish, stirring well to blend. Adjust the seasonings to taste. Cover with aluminum foil.
3. BAKE, covered, for 30 minutes, or until the rice and vegetables are almost cooked. Remove from the oven, uncover, and let stand for 10 minutes to complete the cooking. Fluff once more and adjust the seasonings before serving.

Slow Cooker Chicken Philly Cheesesteak Sandwich

Servings: 4
Cooking Time: 2 Minutes

Ingredients:
- 1 3/4 to 2 pounds chicken tenders
- 2 large green peppers, cut in strips
- 2 medium onions, sliced
- 1 1/2 tablespoons rotisserie seasoning
- 1/2 teaspoon salt
- 4 tablespoons Italian salad dressing

- 4 hoagie rolls, split
- 4 slices Cheddar or American cheese
- 1/4 cup banana pepper rings, optional
- Hot Sauce or ketchup, optional

Directions:

1. In slow cooker crock, combine chicken tenders, pepper strips and onion slices with rotisserie seasoning and salt.

2. Cook on HIGH for 2 to 2 1/2 hours or LOW for 4 to 5 hours.

3. Preheat the toaster oven broiler. Open rolls and place on a cookie sheet

4. Slice chicken tenders. Place back in slow cooker. With a slotted spoon, divide chicken, peppers and onions among rolls and drizzle with Italian dressing. Top with cheese slices.

5. Place under broiler until cheese is melted, about 2 minutes.

6. Serve with banana peppers, hot sauce or ketchup, if desired.

Light Beef Stroganoff

Servings: 4
Cooking Time: 40 Minutes

Ingredients:
- Sauce:
- 1 cup skim milk
- 1 cup fat-free half-and-half
- 2 tablespoons reduced-fat cream cheese, at room temperature
- 4 tablespoons unbleached flour
- 2 pounds lean round or sirloin steak, cut into strips 2 inches long and ½ inch thick
- Browning mixture:
- 1 tablespoon soy sauce
- 2 tablespoons spicy brown mustard
- 1 tablespoon olive oil

- 2 teaspoons garlic powder
- Salt and freshly ground black pepper to taste

Directions:

1. Whisk together the sauce ingredients in a medium bowl until smooth. Set aside.

2. Combine the beef strips and browning mixture ingredients in an oiled or nonstick 8½ × 8½ × 2-inch square baking (cake) pan.

3. BROIL for 8 minutes, or until the strips are browned, turning with tongs after 4 minutes. Transfer to a 1-quart 8½ × 8½ × 4-inch ovenproof baking dish. Add the sauce and mix well. Adjust the seasonings to taste. Cover with aluminum foil.

4. BAKE, covered, for 40 minutes, or until the meat is tender.

Glazed Pork Tenderloin With Carrots Sheet Pan Supper

Servings: 4-6
Cooking Time: 20 Minutes

Ingredients:
- 1 pound pork tenderloin
- 1 teaspoon steak seasoning blend
- 2 large carrots, sliced 1/2-inch thick
- 2 large parsnips, sliced 1/2-inch thick
- 1/2 small sweet onion, cut in thin wedges
- 1 tablespoon olive oil
- Salt and pepper to taste
- 1/2 cup apricot jam
- 1 tablespoon balsamic vinegar

Directions:

1. Place rack on bottom position of toaster oven. Heat the toaster oven to 425°F. Spray the toaster oven baking pan with nonstick cooking spray or line the pan with nonstick aluminum foil.

2. Place pork tenderloin diagonally in center of pan. Sprinkle pork with seasoning blend.

3. In a large bowl, combine carrots, parsnips and onion. Add olive oil, salt and black pepper and stir until vegetables are coated. Arrange vegetables evenly in pan around pork.

4. Bake 20 minutes. Stir vegetables.

5. Meanwhile, in a small bowl, combine apricot jam and balsamic vinegar. Spoon about half of mixture over pork.

6. Continue baking until pork reaches reaches 160°F when tested with a meat thermometer and vegetables are roasted, about 10 minutes. Slice pork and serve with remaining sauce, if desired.

Sheet Pan Beef Fajitas

Servings: 3
Cooking Time: 10 Minutes

Ingredients:
- Nonstick cooking spray
- 3 tablespoons olive oil
- 1 ½ teaspoons chili powder
- 2 teaspoons ground cumin
- 1 teaspoon kosher salt
- 1 onion, halved and sliced into ¼-inch strips
- 1 large red or green bell pepper, cut into thin strips
- ¾-pound flank steak, cut across the grain into thin strips
- 3 tablespoons fresh lime juice
- 3 cloves garlic, minced
- 6 flour or corn tortillas, warmed

Directions:
1. Position the rack to broil. Preheat the toaster oven on the Broil setting. Spray a 12 x 12-inch baking pan with nonstick cooking spray.

2. Combine the olive oil, chili powder, cumin, and salt in a small bowl. Add the onion and bell pepper and toss to coat them evenly with the mixture. Use a slotted spoon to remove the vegetables from the seasoned oil mixture. Reserve the seasoned oil mixture. Place the vegetables in a single layer on the prepared pan. Broil for about 5 minutes or until the vegetables are beginning to brown.

3. Meanwhile, toss the steak strips in the reserved seasoned oil mixture. Push the vegetables to one side of the pan and add the steak in a single layer on the other side of the pan. Broil for 5 minutes.

4. When the meat is done, remove the meat from the pan and toss with the lime juice and garlic. Serve the meat and vegetables in warm tortillas.

Roasted Harissa Chicken + Vegetables

Servings: 4
Cooking Time: 30 Minutes

Ingredients:
- Nonstick cooking spray
- 1 medium zucchini, halved lengthwise and sliced crosswise ½ inch thick
- ½ large red onion, sliced ¼ inch thick
- 2 tablespoons olive oil
- Kosher salt and freshly ground black pepper
- 1 pound boneless, skinless chicken breasts, cut into 1-inch cubes
- ½ teaspoon ground cumin
- 1 clove garlic, minced
- 2 tablespoons harissa sauce or paste
- 1 tablespoon honey
- 2 tablespoons minced fresh cilantro

- 2 cups hot cooked rice
- Optional toppings: plain Greek yogurt or sour cream, sesame seeds (toasted or chopped), or dry-roasted peanuts

Directions:

1. Preheat the toaster oven to 400°F. Spray a 12 x 12-inch baking pan with nonstick cooking spray.
2. Place the zucchini and red onion in a medium bowl. Drizzle with 1 tablespoon olive oil and season with salt and pepper. Stir to coat the vegetables evenly. Arrange the vegetables in a single layer in the prepared baking pan. Roast, uncovered, for 10 minutes.
3. Place the chicken cubes in that same bowl. Drizzle with the remaining 1 tablespoon olive oil. Season with the cumin, garlic, salt, and pepper. Stir to coat the chicken evenly.
4. Stir the vegetables and move to one side of the pan. Arrange the chicken in a single layer on the other side of the pan. Roast for 10 minutes.
5. Blend the harissa and honey in a small bowl. Drizzle the sauce over the chicken and vegetables. Using a pastry brush, coat the chicken and vegetables evenly. Roast, uncovered, for an additional 8 to 10 minutes, or until the vegetables are tender and the chicken registers 165°F on a meat thermometer.
6. Spoon the chicken, vegetables, and any collected liquid onto a serving platter. Sprinkle with the cilantro. Serve the chicken and vegetables with the rice and, if desired, a dollop of plain Greek yogurt and a sprinkling of sesame seeds.

Chicken Tortilla Roll-ups

Servings: 4
Cooking Time: 10 Minutes

Ingredients:

- Nonstick cooking spray
- ¼ cup olive oil
- 2 cloves garlic, minced
- 1 ½ cups shredded cooked chicken
- 1 cup shredded Mexican blend or cheddar cheese
- ½ cup frozen corn, thawed
- ⅓ cup salsa verde
- 1 green onion, white and green portions, chopped
- 2 tablespoons minced fresh cilantro
- 1 tablespoon fresh lime juice
- ½ teaspoon ground cumin
- ¼ teaspoon Sriracha or hot sauce
- Kosher salt and freshly ground black pepper
- 8 flour tortillas, about 8 inches in diameter
- Optional toppings: minced cilantro, salsa, guacamole, sour cream

Directions:

1. Preheat the toaster oven to 375°F. Spray a 12 x 12-inch baking pan with nonstick cooking spray.
2. Stir the oil and garlic in a small bowl; set aside.
3. Stir the chicken, cheese, corn, salsa verde, green onion, cilantro, lime juice, cumin, and Sriracha in a large bowl. Season with salt and pepper.
4. Brush both sides of a tortilla very lightly with the garlic oil. Spoon about ⅓ cup chicken filling on the lower side of the tortilla. Roll the tortilla over the filling. Place the filled tortilla, seam side down, in the prepared baking pan. Repeat with the remaining tortillas and filling.
5. Brush the tops of each filled tortilla with the remaining garlic oil, coating them evenly and especially covering the edges of the tortillas.
6. Bake, uncovered, for 10 minutes or until the tortillas are crisp and the filling is hot. Serve with your choice of any of the various toppings.

Italian Baked Stuffed Tomatoes

Servings: 4
Cooking Time: 30 Minutes

Ingredients:

- 4 large tomatoes
- 1 cup shredded chicken
- 1 1/2 cup shredded mozzarella, divided
- 1 1/2 cup cooked rice
- 2 tablespoon minced onion
- 1/4 cup grated parmesan cheese
- 1 tablespoon dried Italian seasoning
- salt
- pepper
- Basil

Directions:

1. Preheat the toaster oven to 350°F. Spray toaster oven pan with nonstick cooking spray.
2. Cut the top off each tomato and scoop centers out. Place bottoms on prepared pan. Chop 3 tomatoes (about 1 1/2 cup, chopped) and add to large bowl.
3. Add shredded chicken, 1 cup shredded mozzarella cheese, rice, onion, Parmesan cheese, Italian seasoning, salt and pepper to large bowl and stir until blended. Divide between tomatoes, about 1 cup per tomato. Top with remaining mozzarella and tomato top.
4. Bake 25 to 30 minutes until cheese is melted and mixture is heated through.
5. Garnish with basil before serving.

Baked Picnic Pinto Beans

Servings: 4
Cooking Time: 40 Minutes

Ingredients:

- 1 tomato, peeled and finely chopped
- 2 15-ounce cans pinto beans, drained
- 6 lean turkey bacon strips, cooked, drained, and crumbled
- 1 cup good-quality dark beer or ale
- 3 tablespoons finely chopped onion
- 1 tablespoon ketchup
- 2 tablespoons molasses
- 1 teaspoon Dijon mustard
- 1 teaspoon Worcestershire sauce
- 1 teaspoon garlic powder
- Salt and butcher's pepper to taste

Directions:

1. Preheat the toaster oven to 375° F.
2. Peel the tomato by immersing it in boiling water for 1 minute. Remove with tongs and when cool enough to handle, pull the skin away with a sharp paring knife. Chop and place in a 1-quart 8½ × 8½ × 4-inch ovenproof baking dish. Add all the other ingredients, stirring to mix well. Adjust the seasonings to taste. Cover with aluminum foil.
3. BAKE, covered, for 40 minutes.

Inspirational Personal Pizza

Servings: 1
Cooking Time: 30 Minutes

Ingredients:

- 1 9-inch ready-made pizza crust
- 1 teaspoon olive oil
- 2 tablespoons tomato paste
- 4 ounces (½ cup) ground lean turkey breast
- 2 tablespoons sliced marinated artichokes
- 2 tablespoons pitted and chopped kalamata olives
- 2 tablespoons crumbled feta cheese
- 1 tablespoon chopped fresh basil leaves
- 1 tablespoon chopped fresh oregano leaves
- 2 tablespoons grated Parmesan cheese

- ¼ teaspoon red pepper flakes

Directions:

1. Preheat the toaster oven to 375°F.

2. Brush the pizza crust with the olive oil and spread on the tomato paste. Add all the other ingredients. Place the pizza on the toaster oven rack.

3. BAKE for 30 minutes, or until the topping is cooked and the crust is lightly browned.

Middle Eastern Roasted Chicken

Servings: 4

Cooking Time: 25 Minutes

Ingredients:

- 3 tablespoons fresh lemon juice
- ¼ cup plus 1 tablespoon olive oil
- 4 cloves garlic, minced
- ½ teaspoon kosher salt
- 1 teaspoon freshly ground black pepper
- 1 teaspoon ground cumin
- 1 teaspoon paprika
- ½ teaspoon turmeric
- ⅛ teaspoon red pepper flakes
- 1 pound boneless, skinless chicken breasts
- 1 large onion, cut into thin wedges

Directions:

1. Whisk the lemon juice, ¼ cup olive oil, garlic, salt, pepper, cumin, paprika, turmeric, and red pepper flakes in a small bowl until blended.

2. Cut the chicken breast lengthwise into thin scaloppine slices. Place the chicken in a nonreactive dish and pour the marinade over the chicken. Turn the chicken to coat thoroughly and evenly. Cover, refrigerate, and marinate for at least 1 hour and up to 10 hours. (The longer the better, as the flavor melds with the chicken.)

3. Remove the chicken from the refrigerator and add the onion to the marinade.

4. Preheat the toaster oven to 425°F. Brush the remaining tablespoon of olive oil over the bottom of a 12 x 12-inch pan. Place the chicken pieces on one side of the baking sheet and the onion wedges on the other side in a single layer. Discard any remaining marinade.

5. Roast for 20 to 25 minutes or until the chicken is browned and a meat thermometer registers 165°F. Remove from the oven and let rest a few minutes, then slice the chicken into thin strips. Toss with the onion and serve.

POULTRY

Chicken Potpie

Servings: 4
Cooking Time: 48 Minutes

Ingredients:
- Pie filling:
- 1 tablespoon unbleached flour
- ½ cup evaporated skim milk
- 4 skinless, boneless chicken thighs, cut into 1-inch cubes
- 1 cup potatoes, peeled and cut into ½-inch pieces
- ½ cup frozen green peas
- ½ cup thinly sliced carrot
- 2 tablespoons chopped onion
- ½ cup chopped celery
- 1 teaspoon garlic powder
- Salt and freshly ground black pepper to taste
- 8 sheets phyllo pastry, thawed Olive oil

Directions:
1. Preheat the toaster oven to 400° F.
2. Whisk the flour into the milk until smooth in a 1-quart 8½ × 8½ × 4-inch ovenproof baking dish. Add the remaining filling ingredients and mix well. Adjust the seasonings to taste. Cover the dish with aluminum foil.
3. BAKE for 40 minutes, or until the carrot, potatoes, and celery are tender. Remove from the oven and uncover.
4. Place one sheet of phyllo pastry on top of the baked pie-filling mixture, bending the edges to fit the shape of the baking dish. Brush the sheet with olive oil. Add another sheet on top of it and brush with oil. Continue adding the remaining sheets, brushing each one, until the crust is completed. Brush the top with oil.
5. BAKE for 6 minutes, or until the phyllo pastry is browned.

Crispy Chicken Tenders

Servings: 4
Cooking Time: 22 Minutes

Ingredients:
- 1 pound boneless, skinless chicken breasts
- ½ cup all-purpose flour
- ½ teaspoon kosher salt
- ¼ teaspoon freshly ground black ground pepper
- 1 large egg, beaten
- 3 tablespoons whole milk
- 1 cup cornflake crumbs
- ½ cup grated Parmesan cheese
- Nonstick cooking spray

Directions:
1. Preheat the toaster oven to 375°F. Line a 12 x 12-inch baking pan with nonstick aluminum foil. (Or if lining the pan with regular foil, spray it with nonstick cooking spray.)
2. Cover the chicken with plastic wrap. Pound the chicken with the flat side of a meat pounder until it is even and about ½ inch thick. Cut the chicken into strips about 1 by 3 inches.
3. Combine the flour, salt, and pepper in a small shallow dish. Place the egg and milk in another small shallow dish and use a fork to combine. Place the cornflake crumbs and Parmesan in a third small shallow dish and combine.
4. Dredge each chicken piece in the flour, then dip in the egg mixture, and then coat with the

cornflake crumb mixture. Place the chicken strips in a single layer in the prepared baking pan. Spray the chicken strips generously with nonstick cooking spray.

5. Bake for 10 minutes. Turn the chicken and spray with nonstick cooking spray. Bake for an additional 10 to 12 minutes, or until crisp and a meat thermometer registers 165 ºF.

Chicken Cutlets With Broccoli Rabe And Roasted Peppers

Servings: 2

Cooking Time: 10 Minutes

Ingredients:

- ½ bunch broccoli rabe
- olive oil, in a spray bottle
- salt and freshly ground black pepper
- ⅔ cup roasted red pepper strips
- 2 (4-ounce) boneless, skinless chicken breasts
- 2 tablespoons all-purpose flour
- 1 egg, beaten
- ⅓ cup seasoned breadcrumbs
- 2 slices aged provolone cheese

Directions:

1. Bring a medium saucepot of salted water to a boil on the stovetop. Blanch the broccoli rabe for 3 minutes in the boiling water and then drain. When it has cooled a little, squeeze out as much water as possible, drizzle a little olive oil on top, season with salt and black pepper and set aside. Dry the roasted red peppers with a clean kitchen towel and set them aside as well.

2. Place each chicken breast between 2 pieces of plastic wrap. Use a meat pounder to flatten the chicken breasts to about ½-inch thick. Season the chicken on both sides with salt and pepper.

3. Preheat the toaster oven to 400°F.

4. Set up a dredging station with three shallow dishes. Place the flour in one dish, the egg in a second dish and the breadcrumbs in a third dish. Coat the chicken on all sides with the flour. Shake off any excess flour and dip the chicken into the egg. Let the excess egg drip off and coat both sides of the chicken in the breadcrumbs. Spray the chicken with olive oil on both sides and transfer to the air fryer oven.

5. Air-fry the chicken at 400°F for 5 minutes. Turn the chicken over and air-fry for another minute. Then, top the chicken breast with the broccoli rabe and roasted peppers. Place a slice of the provolone cheese on top and secure it with a toothpick or two.

6. Air-fry at 360° for 3 to 4 minutes to melt the cheese and warm everything together.

Pickle Brined Fried Chicken

Servings: 4

Cooking Time: 47 Minutes

Ingredients:

- 4 bone-in, skin-on chicken legs, cut into drumsticks and thighs (about 3½ pounds)
- pickle juice from a 24-ounce jar of kosher dill pickles
- ½ cup flour
- salt and freshly ground black pepper
- 2 eggs
- 1 cup fine breadcrumbs
- 1 teaspoon salt
- 1 teaspoon freshly ground black pepper
- ½ teaspoon ground paprika
- ⅛ teaspoon ground cayenne pepper
- vegetable or canola oil in a spray bottle

Directions:

1. Place the chicken in a shallow dish and pour the pickle juice over the top. Cover and transfer the chicken to the refrigerator to brine in the pickle juice for 3 to 8 hours.

2. When you are ready to cook, remove the chicken from the refrigerator to let it come to room temperature while you set up a dredging station. Place the flour in a shallow dish and season well with salt and freshly ground black pepper. Whisk the eggs in a second shallow dish. In a third shallow dish, combine the breadcrumbs, salt, pepper, paprika and cayenne pepper.

3. Preheat the toaster oven to 370°F.

4. Remove the chicken from the pickle brine and gently dry it with a clean kitchen towel. Dredge each piece of chicken in the flour, then dip it into the egg mixture, and finally press it into the breadcrumb mixture to coat all sides of the chicken. Place the breaded chicken on a plate or baking sheet and spray each piece all over with vegetable oil.

5. Air-fry the chicken in two batches. Place two chicken thighs and two drumsticks into the air fryer oven. Air-fry for 10 minutes. Then, gently turn the chicken pieces over and air-fry for another 10 minutes. Remove the chicken pieces and let them rest on plate – do not cover. Repeat with the second batch of chicken, air-frying for 20 minutes, turning the chicken over halfway through.

6. Lower the temperature of the air fryer oven to 340°F. Place the first batch of chicken on top of the second batch already in the air fryer oven and air-fry for an additional 7 minutes. Serve warm and enjoy.

Coconut Chicken With Apricot-ginger Sauce

Servings: 4

Cooking Time: 8 Minutes

Ingredients:

- 1½ pounds boneless, skinless chicken tenders, cut in large chunks (about 1¼ inches)
- salt and pepper
- ½ cup cornstarch
- 2 eggs
- 1 tablespoon milk
- 3 cups shredded coconut (see below)
- oil for misting or cooking spray
- Apricot-Ginger Sauce
- ½ cup apricot preserves
- 2 tablespoons white vinegar
- ¼ teaspoon ground ginger
- ¼ teaspoon low-sodium soy sauce
- 2 teaspoons white or yellow onion, grated or finely minced

Directions:

1. Mix all ingredients for the Apricot-Ginger Sauce well and let sit for flavors to blend while you cook the chicken.

2. Season chicken chunks with salt and pepper to taste.

3. Place cornstarch in a shallow dish.

4. In another shallow dish, beat together eggs and milk.

5. Place coconut in a third shallow dish. (If also using panko breadcrumbs, as suggested below, stir them to mix well.)

6. Spray air fryer oven with oil or cooking spray.

7. Dip each chicken chunk into cornstarch, shake off excess, and dip in egg mixture.

8. Shake off excess egg mixture and roll lightly in coconut or coconut mixture. Spray with oil.

9. Place coated chicken chunks in air fryer oven in a single layer, close together but without sides touching.

10. Air-fry at 360°F for 4 minutes, stop, and turn chunks over.

11. Cook an additional 4 minutes or until chicken is done inside and coating is crispy brown.

12. Repeat steps 9 through 11 to cook remaining chicken chunks.

Chicken Schnitzel Dogs

Servings: 4
Cooking Time: 10 Minutes

Ingredients:
- ½ cup flour
- ½ teaspoon salt
- 1 teaspoon marjoram
- 1 teaspoon dried parsley flakes
- ½ teaspoon thyme
- 1 egg
- 1 teaspoon lemon juice
- 1 teaspoon water
- 1 cup breadcrumbs
- 4 chicken tenders, pounded thin
- oil for misting or cooking spray
- 4 whole-grain hotdog buns
- 4 slices Gouda cheese
- 1 small Granny Smith apple, thinly sliced
- ½ cup shredded Napa cabbage
- coleslaw dressing

Directions:
1. In a shallow dish, mix together the flour, salt, marjoram, parsley, and thyme.
2. In another shallow dish, beat together egg, lemon juice, and water.
3. Place breadcrumbs in a third shallow dish.

4. Cut each of the flattened chicken tenders in half lengthwise.

5. Dip flattened chicken strips in flour mixture, then egg wash. Let excess egg drip off and roll in breadcrumbs. Spray both sides with oil or cooking spray.

6. Air-fry at 390°F for 5 minutes. Spray with oil, turn over, and spray other side.

7. Air-fry for 3 to 5 minutes more, until well done and crispy brown.

8. To serve, place 2 schnitzel strips on bottom of each hot dog bun. Top with cheese, sliced apple, and cabbage. Drizzle with coleslaw dressing and top with other half of bun.

Orange-glazed Roast Chicken

Servings: 6
Cooking Time: 100 Minutes

Ingredients:
- 1 3-pound whole chicken, rinsed and patted dry with paper towels
- Brushing mixture:
- 2 tablespoons orange juice concentrate
- 1 tablespoon soy sauce
- 1 tablespoon toasted sesame oil
- 1 teaspoon ground ginger
- Salt and freshly ground black pepper to taste

Directions:
1. Preheat the toaster oven to 400° F.
2. Place the chicken, breast side up, in an oiled or nonstick 8½ × 8½ × 2-inch square (cake) pan and brush with the mixture, which has been combined in a small bowl, reserving the remaining mixture. Cover with aluminum foil.
3. BAKE for 1 hour and 20 minutes. Uncover and brush the chicken with remaining mixture.
4. BAKE, uncovered, for 20 minutes, or until the breast is tender when pierced with a fork and golden brown.

Quick Chicken For Filling

Servings: 2

Cooking Time: 8 Minutes

Ingredients:

- 1 pound chicken tenders, skinless and boneless
- ½ teaspoon ground cumin
- ½ teaspoon garlic powder
- cooking spray

Directions:

1. Sprinkle raw chicken tenders with seasonings.
2. Spray air fryer oven lightly with cooking spray to prevent sticking.
3. Place chicken in air fryer oven in single layer.
4. Air-fry at 390°F for 4 minutes, turn chicken strips over, and air-fry for an additional 4 minutes.
5. Test for doneness. Thick tenders may require an additional minute or two.

Roasted Game Hens With Vegetable Stuffing

Servings: 2

Cooking Time: 50 Minutes

Ingredients:

- Stuffing:
- 1 cup multigrain bread crumbs
- 2 tablespoons chopped onion
- 1 carrot, shredded
- 1 celery stalk, shredded
- 1 garlic clove, minced
- 2 tablespoons chopped fresh parsley
- Salt and freshly ground black pepper to taste
- 2 whole game hens (thawed or fresh), giblets removed, rinsed, and patted dry with paper towels

Directions:

1. Preheat the toaster oven to 350° F.
2. Combine the stuffing ingredients in a medium bowl. Stuff the cavities of the game hens and place them in a baking dish.
3. BAKE, covered, for 45 minutes, or until the meat is tender and the juices run clear when the breast is pierced with a fork.
4. BROIL, uncovered, for 8 minutes, or until lightly browned.

Curry Powder

Servings: 1

Cooking Time: 5 Minutes

Ingredients:

- ½ cup coriander seeds
- 2 tablespoons ground cumin
- 2 tablespoons black peppercorns
- 1 tablespoon sesame seeds
- 1 tablespoon cardamom seeds, extracted from the pods
- 2 small dried chili peppers
- 3 tablespoons turmeric
- 2 tablespoons ground ginger

Directions:

1. Combine the coriander seeds, cumin, peppercorns, sesame seeds, cardamom seeds, and chili peppers in an oiled or nonstick 8½ × 8½ × 2-inch square baking (cake) pan.
2. TOAST once, then turn with tongs and toast again, or continue toasting and turning until evenly toasted. Cool and grind the spices in a blender until the mixture becomes a powder. Add the turmeric and ground ginger and mix well. Store in a covered container in the refrigerator.

Fiesta Chicken Plate

Servings: 4

Cooking Time: 15 Minutes

Ingredients:

- 1 pound boneless, skinless chicken breasts (2 large breasts)
- 2 tablespoons lime juice
- 1 teaspoon cumin
- ½ teaspoon salt
- ½ cup grated Pepper Jack cheese
- 1 16-ounce can refried beans
- ½ cup salsa
- 2 cups shredded lettuce
- 1 medium tomato, chopped
- 2 avocados, peeled and sliced
- 1 small onion, sliced into thin rings
- sour cream
- tortilla chips (optional)

Directions:

1. Split each chicken breast in half lengthwise.

2. Mix lime juice, cumin, and salt together and brush on all surfaces of chicken breasts.

3. Place in air fryer oven and air-fry at 390°F for 15 minutes, until well done.

4. Divide the cheese evenly over chicken breasts and air-fry for an additional minute to melt cheese.

5. While chicken is cooking, heat refried beans on stovetop or in microwave.

6. When ready to serve, divide beans among 4 plates. Place chicken breasts on top of beans and spoon salsa over. Arrange the lettuce, tomatoes, and avocados artfully on each plate and scatter with the onion rings.

7. Pass sour cream at the table and serve with tortilla chips if desired.

Guiltless Bacon

Servings: 4

Cooking Time: 10 Minutes

Ingredients:

- 6 slices lean turkey bacon, placed on a broiling pan

Directions:

1. BROIL 5 minutes, turn the pieces, and broil again for 5 more minutes, or until done to your preference. Press the slices between paper towels and serve immediately.

Buffalo Egg Rolls

Servings: 8

Cooking Time: 9 Minutes

Ingredients:

- 1 teaspoon water
- 1 tablespoon cornstarch
- 1 egg
- 2½ cups cooked chicken, diced or shredded (see opposite page)
- ⅓ cup chopped green onion
- ⅓ cup diced celery
- ⅓ cup buffalo wing sauce
- 8 egg roll wraps
- oil for misting or cooking spray
- Blue Cheese Dip
- 3 ounces cream cheese, softened
- ⅓ cup blue cheese, crumbled
- 1 teaspoon Worcestershire sauce
- ¼ teaspoon garlic powder
- ¼ cup buttermilk (or sour cream)

Directions:

1. Mix water and cornstarch in a small bowl until dissolved. Add egg, beat well, and set aside.

2. In a medium size bowl, mix together chicken, green onion, celery, and buffalo wing sauce.

3. Divide chicken mixture evenly among 8 egg roll wraps, spooning ½ inch from one edge.

4. Moisten all edges of each wrap with beaten egg wash.

5. Fold the short ends over filling, then roll up tightly and press to seal edges.

6. Brush outside of wraps with egg wash, then spritz with oil or cooking spray.

7. Place 4 egg rolls in air fryer oven.

8. Air-fry at 390°F for 9 minutes or until outside is brown and crispy.

9. While the rolls are cooking, prepare the Blue Cheese Dip. With a fork, mash together cream cheese and blue cheese.

10. Stir in remaining ingredients.

11. Dip should be just thick enough to slightly cling to egg rolls. If too thick, stir in buttermilk or milk 1 tablespoon at a time until you reach the desired consistency.

12. Cook remaining 4 egg rolls as in steps 7 and 8.

13. Serve while hot with Blue Cheese Dip, more buffalo wing sauce, or both.

Fried Chicken

Servings: 4
Cooking Time: 40 Minutes

Ingredients:
- 12 skin-on chicken drumsticks
- 1 cup buttermilk
- 1½ cups all-purpose flour
- 1 tablespoon smoked paprika
- ¾ teaspoon celery salt
- ¾ teaspoon dried mustard
- ½ teaspoon garlic powder
- ½ teaspoon freshly ground black pepper
- ½ teaspoon sea salt
- ½ teaspoon dried thyme
- ¼ teaspoon dried oregano
- 4 large eggs
- Oil spray (hand-pumped)

Directions:
1. Place the chicken and buttermilk in a medium bowl, cover, and refrigerate for at least 1 hour, up to overnight.

2. Preheat the toaster oven to 375°F on AIR FRY for 5 minutes.

3. In a large bowl, stir the flour, paprika, celery salt, mustard, garlic powder, pepper, salt, thyme, and oregano until well mixed.

4. Beat the eggs until frothy in a medium bowl and set them beside the flour.

5. Place the air-fryer basket in the baking tray and generously spray it with the oil.

6. Dredge a chicken drumstick in the flour, then the eggs, and then in the flour again, thickly coating it, and place the drumstick in the basket. Repeat with 5 more drumsticks and spray them all lightly with the oil on all sides.

7. In position 2, air fry for 20 minutes, turning halfway through, until golden brown and crispy with an internal temperature of 165°F.

8. Repeat with the remaining chicken, covering the cooked chicken loosely with foil to keep it warm. Serve.

Crispy Fried Onion Chicken Breasts

Servings: 2
Cooking Time: 13 Minutes

Ingredients:
- ¼ cup all-purpose flour
- salt and freshly ground black pepper

- 1 egg
- 2 tablespoons Dijon mustard
- 1½ cups crispy fried onions (like French's®)
- ½ teaspoon paprika
- 2 (5-ounce) boneless, skinless chicken breasts
- vegetable or olive oil, in a spray bottle

Directions:

1. Preheat the toaster oven to 380°F.

2. Set up a dredging station with three shallow dishes. Place the flour in the first shallow dish and season well with salt and freshly ground black pepper. Combine the egg and Dijon mustard in a second shallow dish and whisk until smooth. Place the fried onions in a sealed bag and using a rolling pin, crush them into coarse crumbs. Combine these crumbs with the paprika in the third shallow dish.

3. Dredge the chicken breasts in the flour. Shake off any excess flour and dip them into the egg mixture. Let any excess egg drip off. Then coat both sides of the chicken breasts with the crispy onions. Press the crumbs onto the chicken breasts with your hands to make sure they are well adhered.

4. Spray or brush the bottom of the air fryer oven with oil. Transfer the chicken breasts to the air fryer oven and air-fry at 380°F for 13 minutes, turning the chicken over halfway through the cooking time.

5. Serve immediately.

Chicken Adobo

Servings: 6
Cooking Time: 12 Minutes

Ingredients:

- 6 boneless chicken thighs
- ¼ cup soy sauce or tamari
- ½ cup rice wine vinegar
- 4 cloves garlic, minced
- ⅛ teaspoon crushed red pepper flakes
- ½ teaspoon black pepper

Directions:

1. Place the chicken thighs into a resealable plastic bag with the soy sauce or tamari, the rice wine vinegar, the garlic, and the crushed red pepper flakes. Seal the bag and let the chicken marinate at least 1 hour in the refrigerator.

2. Preheat the toaster oven to 400°F.

3. Drain the chicken and pat dry with a paper towel. Season the chicken with black pepper and liberally spray with cooking spray.

4. Place the chicken in the air fryer oven and air-fry for 9 minutes, turn over at 9 minutes and check for an internal temperature of 165°F, and cook another 3 minutes.

Golden Seasoned Chicken Wings

Servings: 2
Cooking Time: 40 Minutes

Ingredients:

- Oil spray (hand-pumped)
- ¾ cup all-purpose flour
- 1 teaspoon garlic powder
- 1 teaspoon smoked paprika
- ½ teaspoon sea salt
- ¼ teaspoon freshly ground black pepper
- ¼ teaspoon onion powder
- 2 pounds chicken wing drumettes and flats

Directions:

1. Preheat the toaster oven to 400°F on AIR FRY for 5 minutes.

2. Place the air-fryer basket in the baking tray and spray it generously with the oil.

3. In a medium bowl, stir the flour, garlic powder, paprika, sea salt, pepper, and onion powder until well mixed.

4. Add half the chicken wings to the bowl and toss to coat with the flour.

5. Arrange the wings in the basket and spray both sides lightly with the oil.

6. In position 2, air fry for 20 minutes, turning halfway through, until golden brown and crispy.

7. Repeat with the remaining wings, covering the cooked wings loosely with foil to keep them warm. Serve.

Honey Lemon Thyme Glazed Cornish Hen

Servings: 2
Cooking Time: 20 Minutes

Ingredients:

- 1 (2-pound) Cornish game hen, split in half
- olive oil
- salt and freshly ground black pepper
- ¼ teaspoon dried thyme
- ¼ cup honey
- 1 tablespoon lemon zest
- juice of 1 lemon
- 1½ teaspoons chopped fresh thyme leaves
- ½ teaspoon soy sauce
- freshly ground black pepper

Directions:

1. Split the game hen in half by cutting down each side of the backbone and then cutting through the breast. Brush or spray both halves of the game hen with the olive oil and then season with the salt, pepper and dried thyme.

2. Preheat the toaster oven to 390°F.

3. Place the game hen, skin side down, into the air fryer oven and air-fry for 5 minutes. Turn the hen halves over and air-fry for 10 minutes.

4. While the hen is cooking, combine the honey, lemon zest and juice, fresh thyme, soy sauce and pepper in a small bowl.

5. When the air fryer oven timer rings, brush the honey glaze onto the game hen and continue to air-fry for another 3 to 5 minutes, just until the hen is nicely glazed, browned and has an internal temperature of 165°F.

6. Let the hen rest for 5 minutes and serve warm.

Nacho Chicken Fries

Servings: 4
Cooking Time: 7 Minutes

Ingredients:

- 1 pound chicken tenders
- salt
- ¼ cup flour
- 2 eggs
- ¾ cup panko breadcrumbs
- ¾ cup crushed organic nacho cheese tortilla chips
- oil for misting or cooking spray
- Seasoning Mix
- 1 tablespoon chili powder
- 1 teaspoon ground cumin
- ½ teaspoon garlic powder
- ½ teaspoon onion powder

Directions:

1. Stir together all seasonings in a small cup and set aside.

2. Cut chicken tenders in half crosswise, then cut into strips no wider than about ½ inch.

3. Preheat the toaster oven to 390°F.

4. Salt chicken to taste. Place strips in large bowl and sprinkle with 1 tablespoon of the seasoning mix. Stir well to distribute seasonings.

5. Add flour to chicken and stir well to coat all sides.

6. Beat eggs together in a shallow dish.

7. In a second shallow dish, combine the panko, crushed chips, and the remaining 2 teaspoons of seasoning mix.

8. Dip chicken strips in eggs, then roll in crumbs. Mist with oil or cooking spray.

9. Chicken strips will cook best if done in two batches. They can be crowded and overlapping a little but not stacked in double or triple layers.

10. Air-fry for 4 minutes. Mist with oil, and cook 3 more minutes, until chicken juices run clear and outside is crispy.

11. Repeat step 10 to cook remaining chicken fries.

Chicken Souvlaki Gyros

Servings: 4
Cooking Time: 18 Minutes

Ingredients:
- ¼ cup extra-virgin olive oil
- 1 clove garlic, crushed
- 1 tablespoon Italian seasoning
- ½ teaspoon paprika
- ½ lemon, sliced
- ¼ teaspoon salt
- 1 pound boneless, skinless chicken breasts
- 4 whole-grain pita breads
- 1 cup shredded lettuce
- ½ cup chopped tomatoes
- ¼ cup chopped red onion
- ¼ cup cucumber yogurt sauce

Directions:

1. In a large resealable plastic bag, combine the olive oil, garlic, Italian seasoning, paprika, lemon, and salt. Add the chicken to the bag and secure shut. Vigorously shake until all the ingredients are combined. Set in the fridge for 2 hours to marinate.

2. When ready to cook, preheat the toaster oven to 360°F.

3. Liberally spray the air fryer oven with olive oil mist. Remove the chicken from the bag and discard the leftover marinade. Place the chicken into the air fryer oven, allowing enough room between the chicken breasts to flip.

4. Air-fry for 10 minutes, flip, and cook another 8 minutes.

5. Remove the chicken from the air fryer oven when it has cooked (or the internal temperature of the chicken reaches 165°F). Let rest 5 minutes. Then thinly slice the chicken into strips.

6. Assemble the gyros by placing the pita bread on a flat surface and topping with chicken, lettuce, tomatoes, onion, and a drizzle of yogurt sauce.

7. Serve warm.

Oven-crisped Chicken

Servings: 4
Cooking Time: 35 Minutes

Ingredients:
- Coating mixture:
- 1 cup cornmeal
- ¼ cup wheat germ
- 1 teaspoon paprika
- 1 teaspoon garlic powder
- Salt and butcher's pepper to taste
- 3 tablespoons olive oil
- 1 tablespoon spicy brown mustard
- 6 skinless, boneless chicken thighs

Directions:

1. Preheat the toaster oven to 375° F.

2. Combine the coating mixture ingredients in a small bowl and transfer to a plate, spreading the mixture evenly over the plate's surface. Set aside.

3. Whisk together the oil and mustard in a bowl. Add the chicken pieces and toss to coat thoroughly. Press both sides of each piece into the coating mixture to coat well. Chill in the refrigerator for 10 minutes. Transfer the chicken pieces to a broiling rack with a pan underneath.

4. BAKE, uncovered, for 35 minutes, or until the meat is tender and the coating is crisp and golden brown or browned to your preference.

Chicken Nuggets

Servings: 20
Cooking Time: 14 Minutes

Ingredients:

- 1 pound boneless, skinless chicken thighs, cut into 1-inch chunks
- ¾ teaspoon salt
- ½ teaspoon black pepper
- ½ teaspoon garlic powder
- ½ teaspoon onion powder
- ½ cup flour
- 2 eggs, beaten
- ½ cup panko breadcrumbs
- 3 tablespoons plain breadcrumbs
- oil for misting or cooking spray

Directions:

1. In the bowl of a food processor, combine chicken, ½ teaspoon salt, pepper, garlic powder, and onion powder. Process in short pulses until chicken is very finely chopped and well blended.

2. Place flour in one shallow dish and beaten eggs in another. In a third dish or plastic bag, mix together the panko crumbs, plain breadcrumbs, and ¼ teaspoon salt.

3. Shape chicken mixture into small nuggets. Dip nuggets in flour, then eggs, then panko crumb mixture.

4. Spray nuggets on both sides with oil or cooking spray and place in air fryer oven in a single layer, close but not overlapping.

5. Air-fry at 360°F for 10 minutes. Spray with oil and cook 4 minutes, until chicken is done and coating is golden brown.

6. Repeat step 5 to cook remaining nuggets.

Pesto-crusted Chicken

Servings: 2
Cooking Time: 31 Minutes

Ingredients:

- Pesto:
- 1 cup fresh cilantro, parsley, and basil leaves
- 3 tablespoons nonfat plain yogurt
- ¼ cup pine nuts, walnut, or pecans
- 3 tablespoons grated Parmesan cheese
- 2 peeled garlic cloves
- 1 tablespoon lemon juice
- 3 tablespoons olive oil
- Salt and freshly ground black pepper to taste
- 2 skinless, boneless chicken breast halves

Directions:

1. Preheat the toaster oven to 450° F.

2. Blend the pesto ingredients in a blender or food processor until smooth. Set aside.

3. Place the chicken breast halves in an oiled or nonstick 8½ × 8½ × 2-inch square (cake) pan. With a butter knife or spatula, spread the mixture liberally on both sides of each chicken breast. Cover the dish with aluminum foil.

4. BAKE, covered, for 25 minutes, or until the chicken is tender. Remove from the oven and uncover.

5. BROIL for 6 minutes, or until the pesto coating is lightly browned.

Spice-rubbed Split Game Hen

Servings: 2
Cooking Time: 48 Minutes

Ingredients:
- Spice rub mixture:
- 1 teaspoon ground cumin
- 1 teaspoon garlic powder
- 1 teaspoon onion powder
- 1 teaspoon paprika
- 1 teaspoon ground coriander
- 1 teaspoon salt (optional)
- 1 Cornish game hen, split

Directions:
1. Preheat the toaster oven to 400° F.

2. Mix all the spices together in a small bowl and rub each half of the game hen well and on both sides to coat evenly. Place the pieces skin side down in a baking dish. Cover the dish with aluminum foil.

3. BAKE for 20 minutes. Turn the pieces over and bake, covered, for another 20 minutes, or until the meat is tender. Remove from the oven and uncover.

4. BROIL 8 minutes, or until browned to your preference.

Italian Baked Chicken

Servings: 4
Cooking Time: 28 Minutes

Ingredients:
- 1 pound boneless, skinless chicken breasts
- ½ cup dry white wine
- 3 tablespoons olive oil
- 2 tablespoons white wine vinegar
- 2 tablespoons fresh lemon juice
- 2 teaspoons Italian seasoning
- 3 cloves garlic, minced
- ½ teaspoon kosher salt
- ¼ teaspoon freshly ground black pepper
- 4 slices salami, cut in half
- 3 tablespoons shredded Parmesan cheese

Directions:
1. If the chicken breasts are large and thick, slice each breast in half lengthwise. Place the chicken in a shallow baking dish.

2. Combine the white wine, olive oil, vinegar, lemon juice, Italian seasoning, garlic, salt, and pepper in a small bowl. Pour over the chicken breasts. Cover and refrigerate for 2 to 8 hours, turning the chicken occasionally to coat.

3. Preheat the toaster oven to 375 °F.

4. Drain the chicken, discarding the marinade, and place the chicken in an ungreased 12 x 12-inch baking pan. Bake, uncovered, for 20 to 25 minutes or until the chicken is done and a meat thermometer registers 165 °F. Place one slice salami (two pieces) on top of each piece of the chicken. Sprinkle the Parmesan evenly over the chicken breasts and broil for 2 to 3 minutes, or until the cheese is melted and starting to brown.

Crispy Chicken Parmesan

Servings: 4
Cooking Time: 12 Minutes

Ingredients:
- 4 skinless, boneless chicken breasts, pounded thin to ¼-inch thickness
- 1 teaspoon salt, divided

- ½ teaspoon black pepper, divided
- 1 cup flour
- 2 eggs
- 1 cup panko breadcrumbs
- ½ teaspoon dried oregano
- ½ cup grated Parmesan cheese

Directions:

1. Pat the chicken breasts with a paper towel. Season the chicken with ½ teaspoon of the salt and ¼ teaspoon of the pepper.

2. In a medium bowl, place the flour.

3. In a second bowl, whisk the eggs.

4. In a third bowl, place the breadcrumbs, oregano, cheese, and the remaining ½ teaspoon of salt and ¼ teaspoon of pepper.

5. Dredge the chicken in the flour and shake off the excess. Dip the chicken into the eggs and then into the breadcrumbs. Set the chicken on a plate and repeat with the remaining chicken pieces.

6. Preheat the toaster oven to 360°F.

7. Place the chicken in the air fryer oven and spray liberally with cooking spray. Air-fry for 8 minutes, turn the chicken breasts over, and cook another 4 minutes. When golden brown, check for an internal temperature of 165°F.

Chicken Chunks

Servings: 4

Cooking Time: 10 Minutes

Ingredients:

- 1 pound chicken tenders cut in large chunks, about 1½ inches
- salt and pepper
- ½ cup cornstarch
- 2 eggs, beaten
- 1 cup panko breadcrumbs
- oil for misting or cooking spray

Directions:

1. Season chicken chunks to your liking with salt and pepper.

2. Dip chicken chunks in cornstarch. Then dip in egg and shake off excess. Then roll in panko crumbs to coat well.

3. Spray all sides of chicken chunks with oil or cooking spray.

4. Place chicken in air fryer oven in single layer and air-fry at 390°F for 5 minutes. Spray with oil, turn chunks over, and spray other side.

5. Air-fry for an additional 5 minutes or until chicken juices run clear and outside is golden brown.

6. Repeat steps 4 and 5 to cook remaining chicken.

BEEF PORK AND LAMB

Slow Cooked Carnitas

Servings: 6

Cooking Time: 360 Minutes

Ingredients:

- 1 pork shoulder (5 pounds), bone-in
- 2½ teaspoons kosher salt
- 1½ teaspoons black pepper
- 1½ teaspoons ground cumin
- 1 teaspoon dried oregano
- ¼ teaspoon ground coriander
- 2 bay leaves
- 6 garlic cloves
- 1 small onion, quartered
- 1 cinnamon stick
- 1 full orange peel (no white)
- 2 oranges, juiced
- 1 lime, juiced

Directions:

1. Season the pork shoulder with salt, pepper, cumin, oregano, and coriander.

2. Place the seasoned pork shoulder in a large pot along with any seasoning that did not stick to the pork.

3. Add in the bay leaves, garlic cloves, onion, cinnamon stick, and orange peel.

4. Squeeze in the juice of two oranges and one lime and cover with foil.

5. Insert the wire rack at low position in the Air Fryer Toaster Oven, then place the pot on the rack.

6. Select the Slow Cook function and press Start/Pause.

7. Remove carefully when done, uncover, and remove the bone.

8. Shred the carnitas and use them in tacos, burritos, or any other way you please.

Perfect Pork Chops

Servings: 3

Cooking Time: 10 Minutes

Ingredients:

- ¾ teaspoon Mild paprika
- ¾ teaspoon Dried thyme
- ¾ teaspoon Onion powder
- ¼ teaspoon Garlic powder
- ¼ teaspoon Table salt
- ¼ teaspoon Ground black pepper
- 3 6-ounce boneless center-cut pork loin chops
- Vegetable oil spray

Directions:

1. Preheat the toaster oven to 400°F.

2. Mix the paprika, thyme, onion powder, garlic powder, salt, and pepper in a small bowl until well combined. Massage this mixture into both sides of the chops. Generously coat both sides of the chops with vegetable oil spray.

3. When the machine is at temperature, set the chops in the air fryer oven with as much air space between them as possible. Air-fry undisturbed for 10 minutes, or until an instant-read meat thermometer inserted into the thickest part of a chop registers 145°F.

4. Use kitchen tongs to transfer the chops to a cutting board or serving plates. Cool for 5 minutes before serving.

Classic Pepperoni Pizza

Servings: 4

Cooking Time: 11 Minutes

Ingredients:

- Oil spray (hand-pumped)
- 1 pound premade pizza dough, or your favorite recipe
- ½ cup store-bought pizza sauce
- ¼ cup grated Parmesan cheese
- ¾ cup shredded mozzarella
- 10 to 12 slices pepperoni
- 2 tablespoons chopped fresh basil
- Pinch red pepper flakes

Directions:

1. Preheat the toaster oven to 425°F on BAKE for 5 minutes.
2. Spray the baking tray with the oil and spread the pizza dough with your fingertips so that it covers the tray. Prick the dough with a fork.
3. In position 2, bake for 8 minutes until the crust is lightly golden.
4. Take the crust out and spread with the pizza sauce, leaving a ½-inch border around the edge. Sprinkle with Parmesan and mozzarella cheeses and arrange the pepperoni on the pizza.
5. Bake for 3 minutes until the cheese is melted and bubbly.
6. Top with the basil and red pepper flakes and serve.

Italian Sausage & Peppers

Servings: 6

Cooking Time: 25 Minutes

Ingredients:

- 1 6-ounce can tomato paste
- ⅔ cup water
- 1 8-ounce can tomato sauce
- 1 teaspoon dried parsley flakes
- ½ teaspoon garlic powder
- ⅛ teaspoon oregano
- ½ pound mild Italian bulk sausage
- 1 tablespoon extra virgin olive oil
- ½ large onion, cut in 1-inch chunks
- 4 ounces fresh mushrooms, sliced
- 1 large green bell pepper, cut in 1-inch chunks
- 8 ounces spaghetti, cooked
- Parmesan cheese for serving

Directions:

1. In a large saucepan or skillet, stir together the tomato paste, water, tomato sauce, parsley, garlic, and oregano. Heat on stovetop over very low heat while preparing meat and vegetables.
2. Break sausage into small chunks, about ½-inch pieces. Place in air fryer oven baking pan.
3. Air-fry at 390°F for 5 minutes. Stir. Cook 7 minutes longer or until sausage is well done. Remove from pan, drain on paper towels, and add to the sauce mixture.
4. If any sausage grease remains in baking pan, pour it off or use paper towels to soak it up. (Be careful handling that hot pan!)
5. Place olive oil, onions, and mushrooms in pan and stir. Air-fry for 5 minutes or just until tender. Using a slotted spoon, transfer onions and mushrooms from baking pan into the sauce and sausage mixture.
6. Place bell pepper chunks in air fryer oven baking pan and air-fry for 8 minutes or until tender. When done, stir into sauce with sausage and other vegetables.
7. Serve over cooked spaghetti with plenty of Parmesan cheese.

Cilantro-crusted Flank Steak

Servings: 2

Cooking Time: 16 Minutes

Ingredients:

- Coating:
- 2 tablespoons chopped onion
- 1 tablespoon olive oil
- 2 tablespoons plain nonfat yogurt
- 1 plum tomato
- ½ cup fresh cilantro leaves
- 2 tablespoons cooking sherry
- ¼ teaspoon hot sauce
- 1 teaspoon garlic powder
- ½ teaspoon chili powder
- Salt and freshly ground black pepper
- 2 8-ounce flank steaks

Directions:

1. Process the coating ingredients in a blender or food processor until smooth. Spread half of the coating mixture on top of the flank steaks. Place the steaks on a broiling rack with a pan underneath.

2. BROIL for 8 minutes. Turn with tongs, spread the remaining mixture on the steaks, and broil again for 8 minutes, or until done to your preference.

Calf's Liver

Servings: 4

Cooking Time: 5 Minutes

Ingredients:

- 1 pound sliced calf's liver
- salt and pepper
- 2 eggs
- 2 tablespoons milk
- ½ cup whole wheat flour
- 1½ cups panko breadcrumbs
- ½ cup plain breadcrumbs
- ½ teaspoon salt
- ¼ teaspoon pepper
- oil for misting or cooking spray

Directions:

1. Cut liver slices crosswise into strips about ½-inch wide. Sprinkle with salt and pepper to taste.

2. Beat together egg and milk in a shallow dish.

3. Place wheat flour in a second shallow dish.

4. In a third shallow dish, mix together panko, plain breadcrumbs, ½ teaspoon salt, and ¼ teaspoon pepper.

5. Preheat the toaster oven to 390°F.

6. Dip liver strips in flour, egg wash, and then breadcrumbs, pressing in coating slightly to make crumbs stick.

7. Cooking half the liver at a time, place strips in air fryer oven in a single layer, close but not touching. Air-fry at 390°F for 5 minutes or until done to your preference.

8. Repeat step 7 to cook remaining liver.

Extra Crispy Country-style Pork Riblets

Servings: 3

Cooking Time: 30 Minutes

Ingredients:

- ⅓ cup Tapioca flour
- 2½ tablespoons Chile powder
- ¾ teaspoon Table salt (optional)
- 1¼ pounds Boneless country-style pork ribs, cut into 1½-inch chunks
- Vegetable oil spray

Directions:

1. Preheat the toaster oven to 375°F .

2. Mix the tapioca flour, chile powder, and salt (if using) in a large bowl until well combined. Add the country-style rib chunks and toss well to coat thoroughly.

3. When the machine is at temperature, gently shake off any excess tapioca coating from the chunks. Generously coat them on all sides with vegetable oil spray. Arrange the chunks in the air fryer oven in one (admittedly fairly tight) layer. The pieces may touch. Air-fry for 30 minutes, rearranging the pieces at the 10- and 20-minute marks to expose any touching bits, until very crisp and well browned.

4. Gently pour the contents of the pan onto a wire rack. Cool for 5 minutes before serving.

Chicken Fried Steak

Servings: 4
Cooking Time: 15 Minutes

Ingredients:
- 2 eggs
- ½ cup buttermilk
- 1½ cups flour
- ¾ teaspoon salt
- ½ teaspoon pepper
- 1 pound beef cube steaks
- salt and pepper
- oil for misting or cooking spray

Directions:
1. Beat together eggs and buttermilk in a shallow dish.

2. In another shallow dish, stir together the flour, ½ teaspoon salt, and ¼ teaspoon pepper.

3. Season cube steaks with remaining salt and pepper to taste. Dip in flour, buttermilk egg wash, and then flour again.

4. Spray both sides of steaks with oil or cooking spray.

5. Cooking in 2 batches, place steaks in air fryer oven in single layer. Air-fry at 360°F for 10 minutes. Spray tops of steaks with oil and cook 5 minutes or until meat is well done.

6. Repeat to cook remaining steaks.

Herbed Lamb Burgers

Servings: 4
Cooking Time: 15 Minutes

Ingredients:
- 1 pound lean ground lamb
- 1 large egg
- 1 tablespoon fresh parsley, chopped
- 2 teaspoons fresh mint, chopped
- 1 teaspoon minced garlic
- ¼ teaspoon sea salt
- ⅛ teaspoon freshly ground black pepper
- Olive oil spray (hand-pumped)
- 4 whole-wheat buns
- ¼ cup store-bought tzatziki sauce
- 1 tomato, cut into slices
- 4 thin red onion slices
- ½ cup shredded lettuce

Directions:
1. Preheat the toaster oven to 350°F on CONVECTION BROIL for 5 minutes.

2. In a large bowl, mix the lamb, egg, parsley, mint, garlic, salt, and pepper. Form the mixture into 4 patties.

3. Place the air-fryer basket in the baking tray and place the burger patties in the basket. Lightly spray the patties with the oil on both sides.

4. In position 2, broil for 15 minutes, turning halfway through.

5. Serve on the buns topped with tzatziki sauce, tomato, onion, and lettuce.

Chipotle-glazed Meat Loaf

Servings: 4

Cooking Time: 65 Minutes

Ingredients:

- 1 ½ pounds lean ground beef
- ¼ cup finely chopped onion
- ½ cup crushed tortilla chips
- 1 teaspoon ground cumin
- ½ teaspoon chili powder
- ½ teaspoon garlic powder
- ½ teaspoon kosher salt
- ¼ teaspoon freshly ground black pepper
- 3 tablespoons chopped pickled jalapeños
- 3 tablespoons chunky salsa
- 1 large egg
- ⅓ cup ketchup
- 3 ½ teaspoons minced chipotle chilies in adobo sauce

Directions:

1. Preheat the toaster oven to 375 ºF. Line a 12 x 12-inch baking pan with aluminum foil.

2. Combine the ground beef, onion, tortilla chips, cumin, chili powder, garlic powder, salt, pepper, pickled jalapeños, salsa, and egg in a large bowl, stirring until blended well. Shape the meat mixture into a 9 x 5-inch loaf and place on the prepared pan.

3. Bake, uncovered, for 30 minutes. Carefully remove the meat loaf from the oven and spoon off any collected grease from the pan.

4. Place the ketchup in a small bowl and stir in the chipotle chilies in adobo sauce. Spread the ketchup mixture on top of the meat loaf. Continue to bake for an additional 25 to 35 minutes or until a meat thermometer registers 160 ºF. Let stand for 10 minutes before slicing.

Indian Fry Bread Tacos

Servings: 4

Cooking Time: 20 Minutes

Ingredients:

- 1 cup all-purpose flour
- 1½ teaspoons salt, divided
- 1½ teaspoons baking powder
- ¼ cup milk
- ¼ cup warm water
- ½ pound lean ground beef
- One 14.5-ounce can pinto beans, drained and rinsed
- 1 tablespoon taco seasoning
- ½ cup shredded cheddar cheese
- 2 cups shredded lettuce
- ¼ cup black olives, chopped
- 1 Roma tomato, diced
- 1 avocado, diced
- 1 lime

Directions:

1. In a large bowl, whisk together the flour, 1 teaspoon of the salt, and baking powder. Make a well in the center and add in the milk and water. Form a ball and gently knead the dough four times. Cover the bowl with a damp towel, and set aside.

2. Preheat the toaster oven to 380°F.

3. In a medium bowl, mix together the ground beef, beans, and taco seasoning. Crumble the meat mixture into the air fryer oven and air-fry for 5 minutes; toss the meat and cook an additional 2 to 3 minutes, or until cooked fully. Place the cooked meat in a bowl for taco assembly; season with the remaining ½ teaspoon salt as desired.

4. On a floured surface, place the dough. Cut the dough into 4 equal parts. Using a rolling pin,

roll out each piece of dough to 5 inches in diameter. Spray the dough with cooking spray and place in the air fryer oven, working in batches as needed. Air-fry for 3 minutes, flip over, spray with cooking spray, and air-fry for an additional 1 to 3 minutes, until golden and puffy.

5. To assemble, place the fry breads on a serving platter. Equally divide the meat and bean mixture on top of the fry bread. Divide the cheese, lettuce, olives, tomatoes, and avocado among the four tacos. Squeeze lime over the top prior to serving.

Kielbasa Chunks With Pineapple & Peppers

Servings: 2
Cooking Time: 10 Minutes

Ingredients:
- ¾ pound kielbasa sausage
- 1 cup bell pepper chunks (any color)
- 1 8-ounce can pineapple chunks in juice, drained
- 1 tablespoon barbeque seasoning
- 1 tablespoon soy sauce
- cooking spray

Directions:
1. Cut sausage into ½-inch slices.
2. In a medium bowl, toss all ingredients together.
3. Spray air fryer oven with nonstick cooking spray.
4. Pour sausage mixture into the air fryer oven.
5. Air-fry at 390°F for approximately 5 minutes. Cook an additional 5 minutes.

Minted Lamb Chops

Servings: 4
Cooking Time: 15 Minutes

Ingredients:
- Mint mixture:
- 4 tablespoons finely chopped fresh mint
- 2 tablespoons nonfat yogurt
- 1 tablespoon olive oil
- Salt and freshly ground black pepper to taste
- 4 lean lamb chops, fat trimmed, approximately ¾ inch thick
- 1 tablespoon balsamic vinegar

Directions:
1. Combine the mint mixture ingredients in a small bowl, stirring well to blend. Set aside. Place the lamp chops on a broiling rack with a pan underneath.
2. BROIL the lamb chops for 10 minutes, or until they are slightly pink. Remove from the oven and brush one side liberally with balsamic vinegar. Turn the chops over with tongs and spread with the mint mixture, using all of the mixture.
3. BROIL again for 5 minutes, or until lightly browned.

Steak Pinwheels With Pepper Slaw And Minneapolis Potato Salad

Servings: 4
Cooking Time: 16 Minutes

Ingredients:
- Brushing mixture:
- ½ cup cold strong brewed coffee
- 2 tablespoons molasses
- 1 tablespoon tomato paste
- 2 garlic cloves, minced
- 1 tablespoon olive oil
- Garlic powder

- 1 teaspoon butcher's pepper
- 1 pound lean, boneless beefsteak, flattened to ⅛-inch thickness with a meat mallet or rolling pin (place steak between 2 sheets of heavy-duty plastic wrap)

Directions:

1. Combine the brushing mixture ingredients in a small bowl and set aside.

2. Cut the steak into 2 × 3-inch strips, brush with the mixture, and roll up, securing the edges with toothpicks. Brush again with the mixture and place in an oiled or nonstick 8½ × 8½ × 2-inch square baking (cake) pan.

3. BROIL for 8 minutes, then turn with tongs, brush with the mixture again, and broil for another 8 minutes, or until browned.

Traditional Pot Roast

Servings: 6
Cooking Time: 75 Minutes

Ingredients:

- 2 tablespoons olive oil
- 1 teaspoon garlic powder
- 1 teaspoon fresh thyme, chopped
- ¼ teaspoon sea salt
- ¼ teaspoon freshly ground black pepper
- 1 (3-pound) beef rump roast

Directions:

1. Preheat the toaster oven to 350°F on CONVECTION BAKE for 5 minutes.

2. In a small bowl, stir the oil, garlic, thyme, salt, and pepper. Spread the mixture all over the beef.

3. Place the air-fryer basket in the baking tray and place the beef in the basket.

4. In position 1, bake for 1 hour and 15 minutes until browned and the internal temperature reaches 145°F for medium.

5. Let the roast rest 10 minutes and serve.

Zesty London Broil

Servings: 4
Cooking Time: 28 Minutes

Ingredients:

- ⅔ cup ketchup
- ¼ cup honey
- ¼ cup olive oil
- 2 tablespoons apple cider vinegar
- 2 tablespoons Worcestershire sauce
- 2 tablespoons minced onion
- ½ teaspoon paprika
- 1 teaspoon salt
- 1 teaspoon freshly ground black pepper
- 2 pounds London broil, top round or flank steak (about 1-inch thick)

Directions:

1. Combine the ketchup, honey, olive oil, apple cider vinegar, Worcestershire sauce, minced onion, paprika, salt and pepper in a small bowl and whisk together.

2. Generously pierce both sides of the meat with a fork or meat tenderizer and place it in a shallow dish. Pour the marinade mixture over the steak, making sure all sides of the meat get coated with the marinade. Cover and refrigerate overnight.

3. Preheat the toaster oven to 400°F.

4. Transfer the London broil to the air fryer oven and air-fry for 28 minutes, depending on how rare or well done you like your steak. Flip the steak over halfway through the cooking time.

5. Remove the London broil from the air fryer oven and let it rest for five minutes on a cutting board. To serve, thinly slice the meat against the grain and transfer to a serving platter.

Stuffed Bell Peppers

Servings: 4

Cooking Time: 10 Minutes

Ingredients:

- ¼ pound lean ground pork
- ¾ pound lean ground beef
- ¼ cup onion, minced
- 1 15-ounce can Red Gold crushed tomatoes
- 1 teaspoon Worcestershire sauce
- 1 teaspoon barbeque seasoning
- 1 teaspoon honey
- ½ teaspoon dried basil
- ½ cup cooked brown rice
- ½ teaspoon garlic powder
- ½ teaspoon oregano
- ½ teaspoon salt
- 2 small bell peppers

Directions:

1. Place pork, beef, and onion in air fryer oven baking pan and air-fry at 360°F for 5 minutes.

2. Stir to break apart chunks and cook 3 more minutes. Continue cooking and stirring in 2-minute intervals until meat is well done. Remove from pan and drain.

3. In a small saucepan, combine the tomatoes, Worcestershire, barbeque seasoning, honey, and basil. Stir well to mix in honey and seasonings.

4. In a large bowl, combine the cooked meat mixture, rice, garlic powder, oregano, and salt. Add ¼ cup of the seasoned crushed tomatoes. Stir until well mixed.

5. Cut peppers in half and remove stems and seeds.

6. Stuff each pepper half with one fourth of the meat mixture.

7. Place the peppers in air fryer oven and air-fry for 10 minutes, until peppers are crisp tender.

8. Heat remaining tomato sauce. Serve peppers with warm sauce spooned over top.

Barbeque Ribs

Servings: 4

Cooking Time: 35 Minutes

Ingredients:

- 2 pounds pork spareribs or baby back ribs, silver skin removed
- 2 tablespoons brown sugar
- 1 teaspoon chili powder
- 1 teaspoon dry mustard
- Sea salt, for seasoning
- Freshly ground black pepper, for seasoning
- Oil spray (hand-pumped)
- 1 cup barbeque sauce

Directions:

1. Preheat the toaster oven to 375°F on AIR FRY for 5 minutes.

2. Cut the ribs into 4 bone sections or to fit in the basket.

3. In a small bowl, combine the brown sugar, chili powder, and mustard, and rub it all over the ribs.

4. Season the ribs with salt and pepper.

5. Place the air-fryer basket in the baking tray and spray it generously with the oil.

6. Arrange the ribs in the basket. There can be overlap if necessary.

7. In position 2, air fry for 35 minutes, turning halfway through, until the ribs are tender, browned, and crisp.

8. Baste the ribs with the barbeque sauce and serve.

Vietnamese Beef Lettuce Wraps

Servings: 4

Cooking Time: 12 Minutes

Ingredients:

- ⅓ cup low-sodium soy sauce
- 2 teaspoons fish sauce
- 2 teaspoons brown sugar
- 1 tablespoon chili paste
- juice of 1 lime
- 2 cloves garlic, minced
- 2 teaspoons fresh ginger, minced
- 1 pound beef sirloin
- Sauce
- ⅓ cup low-sodium soy sauce
- juice of 2 limes
- 1 tablespoon mirin wine
- 2 teaspoons chili paste
- Serving
- 1 head butter lettuce
- ½ cup julienned carrots
- ½ cup julienned cucumber
- ½ cup sliced radishes, sliced into half moons
- 2 cups cooked rice noodles
- ⅓ cup chopped peanuts

Directions:

1. Combine the soy sauce, fish sauce, brown sugar, chili paste, lime juice, garlic and ginger in a bowl. Slice the beef into thin slices, then cut those slices in half. Add the beef to the marinade and marinate for 1 to 3 hours in the refrigerator. When you are ready to cook, remove the steak from the refrigerator and let it sit at room temperature for 30 minutes.

2. Preheat the toaster oven to 400°F.

3. Transfer the beef and marinade to the air fryer oven. Air-fry at 400°F for 12 minutes.

4. While the beef is cooking, prepare a wrap-building station. Combine the soy sauce, lime juice, mirin wine and chili paste in a bowl and transfer to a little pouring vessel. Separate the lettuce leaves from the head of lettuce and put them in a serving bowl. Place the carrots, cucumber, radish, rice noodles and chopped peanuts all in separate serving bowls.

5. When the beef has finished cooking, transfer it to another serving bowl and invite your guests to build their wraps. To build the wraps, place some beef in a lettuce leaf and top with carrots, cucumbers, some rice noodles and chopped peanuts. Drizzle a little sauce over top, fold the lettuce around the ingredients and enjoy!

Tuscan Pork Tenderloin

Servings: 4

Cooking Time: 35 Minutes

Ingredients:

- Nonstick cooking spray.
- 1 pork tenderloin (1 ¼ to 1 ½ pounds)
- Kosher salt and freshly ground black pepper
- 8 to 10 fresh basil leaves
- 1 ½ teaspoons minced garlic (about 3 cloves garlic)
- 2 slices prosciutto
- 2 ounces mozzarella cheese, cut into thin strips, or ½ cup shredded
- 1 tablespoon olive oil
- 1 teaspoon Italian seasoning

Directions:

1. Preheat the toaster oven to 400°F. Spray a 12 x 12-inch baking pan with nonstick cooking spray.

2. Cut the pork tenderloin in half lengthwise, not quite cutting through one side, and gently open it (like a book) so it lays flat. Cover the meat

with plastic wrap. Pound the meat with the flat side of a meat pounder until the meat is even and about ½ inch thick.

3. Season the cut side of the meat with salt and pepper. Arrange the basil leaves evenly over the meat, then sprinkle with 1 teaspoon of the minced garlic. Top with an even layer of prosciutto and cheese. Roll the meat from the longer side covering the cheese and other filling ingredients completely. Tie the meat shut with kitchen twine, taking care to keep the roll tight and the filling inside.

4. Rub the outside of the meat with the olive oil. Mix the Italian seasoning and the remaining ½ teaspoon garlic in a small bowl. Season with salt and pepper. Rub the seasoning mixture evenly over the meat.

5. Place the meat in the prepared pan. Roast, uncovered, for 25 to 35 minutes or until the tenderloin is brown and the pork is just slightly pink inside.

6. Let stand for 5 to 10 minutes. Slice crosswise into slices about 1 inch thick.

Seasoned Boneless Pork Sirloin Chops

Servings: 2
Cooking Time: 16 Minutes

Ingredients:

- Seasoning mixture:
- ½ teaspoon ground cumin
- ¼ teaspoon turmeric
- Pinch of ground cardamom
- Pinch of grated nutmeg
- 1 teaspoon vegetable oil
- 1 teaspoon Pickapeppa sauce
- 2½- to ¾-pound boneless lean pork sirloin chops

Directions:

1. Combine the seasoning mixture ingredients in a small bowl and brush on both sides of the chops. Place the chops on the broiling rack with a pan underneath.

2. BROIL 8 minutes, remove the chops, turn, and brush with the mixture. Broil again for 8 minutes, or until the chops are done to your preference.

Beef Vegetable Stew

Servings: 4
Cooking Time: 120 Minutes

Ingredients:

- 1 pound lean stewing beef, cut into 1-inch chunks
- 2 carrots, diced
- 2 celery stalks
- 1 large potato, diced
- ½ sweet onion, chopped
- 2 teaspoons minced garlic
- 1 (15-ounce) can diced tomatoes, with juices
- 1 teaspoon sea salt
- ½ teaspoon freshly ground black pepper
- 1 cup low-sodium beef broth
- 3 tablespoons all-purpose flour
- 1 cup frozen peas

Directions:

1. Place the rack in position 1 and preheat the toaster oven to 375°F on BAKE for 5 minutes.

2. In a 1½-quart casserole dish, combine the beef, carrots, celery, potato, onion, garlic, tomatoes, salt, and pepper.

3. In a small bowl, stir the broth and flour until well combined. Add the broth mixture to the beef mixture and stir to combine.

4. Cover with foil or a lid and bake for 2 hours, stirring each time you reset the timer, until the meat is very tender.

5. Stir in the peas and let stand for 10 minutes. Serve.

Steak With Herbed Butter

Servings: 2

Cooking Time: 16 Minutes

Ingredients:

- 4 tablespoons unsalted butter, softened
- 1 tablespoon minced flat-leaf (Italian) parsley
- 1 tablespoon chopped fresh chives
- 2 cloves garlic, minced
- 1 teaspoon Worcestershire sauce
- 2 beef strip steaks, cut about 1 ½ inches thick
- 1 tablespoon olive oil
- Kosher salt and freshly ground black pepper

Directions:

1. Combine the butter, parsley, chives, garlic, and Worcestershire sauce in a small bowl until well blended; set aside.

2. Preheat the toaster oven to broil.

3. Brush the steaks with olive oil and season with salt and pepper. Place the steak on the broiler rack set over the broiler pan. Place the pan in the toaster oven, positioning the steaks about 3 to 4 inches below the heating element. (Depending on your oven and the thickness of the steak, you may need to set the rack to the middle position.) Broil for 6 minutes, turn the steaks over, and broil for an additional 7 minutes. If necessary to reach the desired doneness, turn the steaks over again and broil for an additional 3 minutes or until you reach your desired doneness.

4. Spread the herb butter generously over the steaks. Allow the steaks to stand for 5 to 10 minutes before slicing and serving.

Almond And Sun-dried Tomato Crusted Pork Chops

Servings: 4

Cooking Time: 10 Minutes

Ingredients:

- ½ cup oil-packed sun-dried tomatoes
- ½ cup toasted almonds
- ¼ cup grated Parmesan cheese
- ½ cup olive oil
- 2 tablespoons water
- ½ teaspoon salt
- freshly ground black pepper
- 4 center-cut boneless pork chops (about 1¼ pounds)

Directions:

1. Place the sun-dried tomatoes into a food processor and pulse them until they are coarsely chopped. Add the almonds, Parmesan cheese, olive oil, water, salt and pepper. Process all the ingredients into a smooth paste. Spread most of the paste (leave a little in reserve) onto both sides of the pork chops and then pierce the meat several times with a needle-style meat tenderizer or a fork. Let the pork chops sit and marinate for at least 1 hour (refrigerate if marinating for longer than 1 hour).

2. Preheat the toaster oven to 370°F.

3. Brush a little olive oil on the bottom of the air fryer oven. Transfer the pork chops into the air fryer oven, spooning a little more of the sun-dried tomato paste onto the pork chops if there are any

gaps where the paste may have been rubbed off. Air-fry the pork chops at 370°F for 10 minutes, turning the chops over halfway through the cooking process.

4. When the pork chops have finished cooking, transfer them to a serving plate and serve with mashed potatoes and vegetables for a hearty meal.

Chinese Pork And Vegetable Non-stir-fry

Servings: 4
Cooking Time: 30 Minutes

Ingredients:
- Seasoning sauce:
- 1 tablespoon soy sauce
- ¼ cup dry white wine
- 1 tablespoon sesame oil
- 1 tablespoon vegetable oil
- 1 teaspoon Chinese five-spice powder
- 2 6-ounce lean boneless pork chops cut into ¼ × 2-inch strips
- 1 1-pound package frozen vegetable mix or 2 cups sliced assorted fresh vegetables: broccoli, carrots, cauliflower, bell pepper, and the like
- 1 4-ounce can mushroom pieces, drained, or ½ cup cleaned and sliced fresh mushrooms
- 2 tablespoons sesame seeds
- 2 tablespoons minced fresh garlic

Directions:
1. Whisk together the seasoning sauce ingredients in a small bowl. Set aside.
2. Combine the pork, vegetables, mushrooms, sesame seeds, and garlic in an oiled or nonstick 8½ × 8½ × 2-inch square baking (cake) pan. Add the seasoning sauce ingredients and toss to coat the pork, vegetables, and mushrooms well.

3. BROIL for 30 minutes, turning with tongs every 8 minutes, until the vegetables and meat are well cooked and lightly browned.

Beef Al Carbon (street Taco Meat)

Servings: 6
Cooking Time: 8 Minutes

Ingredients:
- 1½ pounds sirloin steak, cut into ½-inch cubes
- ¾ cup lime juice
- ½ cup extra-virgin olive oil
- 1 teaspoon ground cumin
- 2 teaspoons garlic powder
- 1 teaspoon salt

Directions:
1. In a large bowl, toss together the steak, lime juice, olive oil, cumin, garlic powder, and salt. Allow the meat to marinate for 30 minutes. Drain off all the marinade and pat the meat dry with paper towels.
2. Preheat the toaster oven to 400°F.
3. Place the meat in the air fryer oven and spray with cooking spray. Cook the meat for 5 minutes, toss the meat, and continue cooking another 3 minutes, until slightly crispy.

Lamb Burger With Feta And Olives

Servings: 3
Cooking Time: 16 Minutes

Ingredients:
- 2 teaspoons olive oil
- ⅓ onion, finely chopped
- 1 clove garlic, minced
- 1 pound ground lamb

- 2 tablespoons fresh parsley, finely chopped
- 1½ teaspoons fresh oregano, finely chopped
- ½ cup black olives, finely chopped
- ⅓ cup crumbled feta cheese
- ½ teaspoon salt
- freshly ground black pepper
- 4 thick pita breads
- toppings and condiments

Directions:

1. Preheat a medium skillet over medium-high heat on the stovetop. Add the olive oil and cook the onion until tender, but not browned – about 4 to 5 minutes. Add the garlic and air-fry for another minute. Transfer the onion and garlic to a mixing bowl and add the ground lamb, parsley, oregano, olives, feta cheese, salt and pepper. Gently mix the ingredients together.

2. Divide the mixture into 3 or 4 equal portions and then form the hamburgers, being careful not to over-handle the meat. One good way to do this is to throw the meat back and forth between your hands like a baseball, packing the meat each time you catch it. Flatten the balls into patties, making an indentation in the center of each patty. Flatten the sides of the patties as well to make it easier to fit them into the air fryer oven.

3. Preheat the toaster oven to 370°F.

4. If you don't have room for all four burgers, air-fry two or three burgers at a time for 8 minutes at 370°F. Flip the burgers over and air-fry for another 8 minutes. If you cooked your burgers in batches, return the first batch of burgers to the air fryer oven for the last two minutes of cooking to re-heat. This should give you a medium-well burger. If you'd prefer a medium-rare burger, shorten the cooking time to about 13 minutes. Remove the burgers to a resting plate and let the burgers rest for a few minutes before dressing and serving.

5. While the burgers are resting, toast the pita breads in the air fryer oven for 2 minutes. Tuck the burgers into the toasted pita breads, or wrap the pitas around the burgers and serve with a tzatziki sauce or some mayonnaise.

Pork Loin

Servings: 8
Cooking Time: 50 Minutes

Ingredients:
- 1 tablespoon lime juice
- 1 tablespoon orange marmalade
- 1 teaspoon coarse brown mustard
- 1 teaspoon curry powder
- 1 teaspoon dried lemongrass
- 2-pound boneless pork loin roast
- salt and pepper
- cooking spray

Directions:

1. Mix together the lime juice, marmalade, mustard, curry powder, and lemongrass.

2. Rub mixture all over the surface of the pork loin. Season to taste with salt and pepper.

3. Spray air fryer oven with nonstick spray and place pork roast diagonally in the pan.

4. Air-fry at 360°F for approximately 50 minutes, until roast registers 130°F on a meat thermometer.

5. Wrap roast in foil and let rest for 10minutes before slicing.

SNACKS APPETIZERS AND SIDES

Chicken Shawarma Bites

Servings: 6
Cooking Time: 22 Minutes

Ingredients:

- 1½ pounds Boneless skinless chicken thighs, trimmed of any fat and cut into 1-inch pieces
- 1½ tablespoons Olive oil
- Up to 1½ tablespoons Minced garlic
- ½ teaspoon Table salt
- ¼ teaspoon Ground cardamom
- ¼ teaspoon Ground cinnamon
- ¼ teaspoon Ground cumin
- ¼ teaspoon Mild paprika
- Up to a ¼ teaspoon Grated nutmeg
- ¼ teaspoon Ground black pepper

Directions:

1. Preheat the toaster oven to 400°F.
2. Mix all the ingredients in a large bowl until the chicken is thoroughly and evenly coated in the oil and spices.
3. When the machine is at temperature, scrape the coated chicken pieces into the air fryer oven and spread them out into one layer as much as you can. Air-fry for 22 minutes, rotate at least three times during cooking to rearrange the pieces, until well browned and crisp.
4. Pour the chicken pieces onto a wire rack. Cool for 5 minutes before serving.

Cheesy Zucchini Squash Casserole

Servings: 12-14
Cooking Time: 30 Minutes

Ingredients:

- 1 Tablespoon olive oil
- 1 medium sweet onion, halved and thinly sliced
- 1 garlic clove, minced
- 1 pound zucchini, thinly sliced
- 1 pound yellow squash, thinly sliced
- 1 large egg
- 1/2 cup sour cream
- 1 cup shredded Cheddar cheese
- 1 cup shredded Swiss cheese
- 1 teaspoon thyme
- 1 teaspoon salt
- 1/2 teaspoon black pepper
- 3/4 cup seasoned panko crumbs
- 1 Tablespoon butter, melted

Directions:

1. Preheat the toaster oven to 350°F.
2. Heat olive oil in large skillet over medium-high heat. Add onion and garlic; cook 2 minutes. Stir in zucchini and yellow squash, cooking an additional 4 minutes or until squash is tender.
3. Beat egg and sour cream in large bowl until well blended. Stir in squash mixture, cheeses, thyme, salt and pepper. Pour into 8x8-inch baking dish.
4. Stir crumbs and butter in small bowl. Sprinkle over squash mixture.
5. Bake 25 to 30 minutes or until crumbs are golden brown and mixture is heated through.

Potato Chips

Servings: 2

Cooking Time: 15 Minutes

Ingredients:

- 2 medium potatoes
- 2 teaspoons extra-light olive oil
- oil for misting or cooking spray
- salt and pepper

Directions:

1. Peel the potatoes.
2. Using a mandoline or paring knife, shave potatoes into thin slices, dropping them into a bowl of water as you cut them.
3. Dry potatoes as thoroughly as possible with paper towels or a clean dish towel. Toss potato slices with the oil to coat completely.
4. Spray air fryer oven with cooking spray and add potato slices.
5. Stir and separate with a fork.
6. Cook 390°F for 5 minutes. Stir and separate potato slices. Cook 5 more minutes. Stir and separate potatoes again. Cook another 5 minutes.
7. Season to taste.

Creamy Parmesan Polenta

Servings: 4

Cooking Time: 60 Minutes

Ingredients:

- 2½ cups boiling water, divided, plus extra as needed
- ½ cup coarse-ground cornmeal
- ½ teaspoon table salt
- Pinch baking soda
- 1 ounce Parmesan cheese, grated (½ cup)
- 1 tablespoon unsalted butter

Directions:

1. Adjust toaster oven rack to middle position and preheat the toaster oven to 325 degrees. Combine 2 cups boiling water, cornmeal, salt, and baking soda in greased 8-inch square baking dish or pan. Transfer dish to oven and bake until water is absorbed and polenta is thickened, 35 to 40 minutes, rotating dish halfway through baking.
2. Remove baking dish from oven. Stir in remaining ½ cup boiling water, then stir in Parmesan and butter until polenta is smooth and creamy. Adjust consistency with extra boiling water as needed. Serve.

Maple-glazed Acorn Squash

Servings: 2

Cooking Time: 30 Minutes

Ingredients:

- 1 acorn squash (1½ pounds), halved pole to pole, seeded, and cut into 8 wedges
- 1 tablespoon vegetable oil
- 1 teaspoon sugar
- ¼ teaspoon plus pinch table salt, divided
- ¼ teaspoon pepper
- 2 tablespoons maple syrup
- 2 tablespoons unsalted butter
- Pinch cayenne pepper
- 1 teaspoon fresh thyme leaves (optional)

Directions:

1. Adjust toaster oven rack to middle position and preheat the toaster oven to 450 degrees. Toss squash, oil, sugar, ¼ teaspoon salt, and pepper together on small rimmed baking sheet, then arrange cut side down in single layer. Roast until bottoms of squash wedges are deep golden brown, 15 to 20 minutes.
2. Meanwhile, microwave maple syrup, butter, cayenne, and remaining pinch salt in bowl,

stirring occasionally, until butter is melted and mixture is slightly thickened, about 90 seconds; cover to keep warm.

3. Remove sheet from oven, and, using spatula, carefully flip squash. Brush with half of glaze and continue to roast until squash is tender and deep golden, 5 to 8 minutes. Carefully flip squash and brush with remaining glaze. Transfer squash to serving platter and sprinkle with thyme, if using. Serve.

Creamy Scalloped Potatoes

Servings: 4
Cooking Time: 58 Minutes

Ingredients:
- Oil spray (hand-pumped)
- 2 tablespoons salted butter
- 1 small onion, finely chopped
- 1 teaspoon minced garlic
- 2 tablespoons all-purpose flour
- 1 cup whole milk
- ½ cup low-sodium chicken broth
- ¼ teaspoon ground nutmeg
- ⅛ teaspoon sea salt
- ⅛ teaspoon freshly ground black pepper
- 1½ pounds russet potatoes, cut into ⅛-inch-thick slices

Directions:
1. Place the rack on position 1 and preheat the toaster oven on BAKE to 350°F for 5 minutes.
2. Lightly spray an 8-inch-square baking dish with oil and set aside.
3. Melt the butter in a medium saucepan over medium-high heat. Sauté the onion and garlic in the butter until softened, about 4 minutes. Add the flour and cook, whisking, for 1 minute.

4. Whisk in the milk and chicken broth until well blended and cook, whisking constantly, until thickened, about 3 minutes. Remove the sauce from the heat and whisk in the nutmeg, salt, and pepper. Set aside.
5. Layer one-third of the potato slices in the baking dish and top with one-third of the sauce. Repeat the layering in thirds, ending with the cream sauce.
6. Cover the dish with aluminum foil and bake for 25 minutes. Remove the foil and bake for an additional 25 minutes until golden brown and the potatoes are tender. Serve.

Loaded Potato Skins

Servings: 8
Cooking Time: 8 Minutes

Ingredients:
- 12 round baby potatoes
- 3 ounces cream cheese
- 4 slices cooked bacon, crumbled or chopped
- 2 green onions, finely chopped
- ½ cup grated cheddar cheese, divided
- ¼ cup sour cream
- 1 tablespoon milk
- 2 teaspoons hot sauce

Directions:
1. Preheat the toaster oven to 320°F.
2. Poke holes into the baby potatoes with a fork. Place the potatoes onto a microwave-safe plate and microwave on high for 4 to 5 minutes, or until soft to squeeze. Let the potatoes cool until they're safe to handle, about 5 minutes.
3. Meanwhile, in a medium bowl, mix together the cream cheese, bacon, green onions, and ¼ cup of the cheddar cheese; set aside.

4. Slice the baby potatoes in half. Using a spoon, scoop out the pulp, leaving enough pulp on the inside to retain the shape of the potato half. Place the potato pulp into the cream cheese mixture and mash together with a fork. Using a spoon, refill the potato halves with filling.

5. Place the potato halves into the air fryer oven and top with the remaining ¼ cup of cheddar cheese.

6. Cook the loaded baked potato bites in batches for 8 minutes.

7. Meanwhile, make the sour cream sauce. In a small bowl, whisk together the sour cream, milk, and hot sauce. Add more hot sauce if desired.

8. When the potatoes have all finished cooking, place them onto a serving platter and serve with sour cream sauce drizzled over the top or as a dip.

Baked Asparagus Fries

Servings: 2-3
Cooking Time: 14 Minutes

Ingredients:
- 1 1/2 cups mayonnaise
- 3/4 cup grated Parmesan cheese
- 2 cloves garlic, minced
- 1 tablespoon dried parsley
- 1 tablespoon Italian seasoning
- 1 teaspoon salt
- 1/2 teaspoon coarse black pepper
- 1/2 pound thick asparagus, trimmed
- 1 cup panko crumbs

Directions:
1. Heat the oven to 425ºF.
2. In a small bowl, combine mayonnaise, Parmesan cheese, garlic, parsley, Italian seasoning, salt and black pepper.

3. Brush asparagus with 3 tablespoons mayonnaise mixture and roll in crumbs. Place asparagus on the baking pan.
4. Bake 12 to 14 minutes or until lightly browned and asparagus are cooked.
5. Serve asparagus with the remaining mayonnaise mixture.

Polenta Fries With Chili-lime Mayo

Servings: 4
Cooking Time: 28 Minutes

Ingredients:
- 2 teaspoons vegetable or olive oil
- ¼ teaspoon paprika
- 1 pound prepared polenta, cut into 3-inch x ½-inch sticks
- salt and freshly ground black pepper
- Chili-Lime Mayo
- ½ cup mayonnaise
- 1 teaspoon chili powder
- ¼ teaspoon ground cumin
- juice of half a lime
- 1 teaspoon chopped fresh cilantro
- salt and freshly ground black pepper

Directions:
1. Preheat the toaster oven to 400°F.
2. Combine the oil and paprika and then carefully toss the polenta sticks in the mixture.
3. Air-fry the polenta fries at 400°F for 15 minutes. Rotate the fries and continue to air-fry for another 13 minutes or until the fries have browned nicely. Season to taste with salt and freshly ground black pepper.
4. To make the chili-lime mayo, combine all the ingredients in a small bowl and stir well.
5. Serve the polenta fries warm with chili-lime mayo on the side for dipping.

Baked Coconut Shrimp With Curried Chutney

Servings: 8-10

Cooking Time: 11 Minutes

Ingredients:

- 1 cup chutney
- 2 Tablespoons sliced green onion
- 1/2 teaspoon ground curry
- 1/2 teaspoon crushed red pepper
- 2 Tablespoons all-purpose flour
- 1 teaspoon salt
- 1 cup panko breadcrumbs
- 3/4 cup sweetened shredded coconut
- 1 egg white
- 1 pound (16 to 20 count) extra jumbo shrimp
- Cilantro

Directions:

1. In a small bowl, stir chutney, green onion, curry and crushed red pepper until blended. Set aside.

2. Preheat the toaster oven to 450°F. Spray a baking pan with nonstick cooking spray. Set aside.

3. In a large resealable plastic bag, combine flour and salt.

4. Add panko breadcrumbs and coconut to bag. Seal and shake to combine.

5. In a medium bowl, whisk egg white until foamy.

6. Dip one shrimp at a time into egg white.

7. Place shrimp in crumb mixture and press mixture onto shrimp until well coated. Arrange in single layer in prepared baking pan.

8. Bake for 9 to 11 minutes or until crumbs are golden brown. Serve with chutney mixture. Garnish with cilantro.

Warm And Salty Edamame

Servings: 4

Cooking Time: 10 Minutes

Ingredients:

- 1 pound Unshelled edamame
- Vegetable oil spray
- ¾ teaspoon Coarse sea salt or kosher salt

Directions:

1. Preheat the toaster oven to 400°F.

2. Place the edamame in a large bowl and lightly coat them with vegetable oil spray. Toss well, spray again, and toss until they are evenly coated.

3. When the machine is at temperature, pour the edamame into the air fryer oven and air-fry, tossing the pan quite often to rearrange the edamame, for 7 minutes, or until warm and aromatic. (Air-fry for 10 minutes if the edamame were frozen and not thawed.)

4. Pour the edamame into a bowl and sprinkle the salt on top. Toss well, then set aside for a couple of minutes before serving with an empty bowl on the side for the pods.

Sweet Potato Casserole

Servings: 4

Cooking Time: 90 Minutes

Ingredients:

- 2 tablespoons packed brown sugar, divided
- ½ teaspoon grated orange zest, divided, plus 1 tablespoon juice
- 1½ pounds sweet potatoes, peeled and cut into 1½-inch pieces
- 2 tablespoons unsalted butter, cut into 4 pieces
- 2 tablespoons heavy cream
- ½ teaspoon table salt

- ¼ teaspoon ground cinnamon
- ⅛ teaspoon pepper
- Pinch cayenne pepper

Directions:

1. Adjust toaster oven rack to middle position and preheat the toaster oven to 400 degrees. Mix 4 teaspoons sugar and ¼ teaspoon orange zest in small bowl until thoroughly combined; set aside.

2. Toss sweet potatoes and remaining 2 teaspoons sugar together in bowl, then spread into even layer on aluminum foil–lined small rimmed baking sheet. Cover sheet tightly with foil and roast until sweet potatoes are tender, 45 to 60 minutes, rotating sheet halfway through roasting. Remove sheet from oven, select broiler function, and heat broiler.

3. Transfer potatoes and any accumulated liquid to food processor. Add butter, cream, salt, cinnamon, pepper, cayenne, remaining ¼ teaspoon orange zest, and orange juice and process until completely smooth, 30 to 60 seconds, scraping down sides of bowl as needed.

4. Transfer potato puree to 8-inch square broiler-safe baking dish or pan and sprinkle evenly with reserved sugar-zest mixture. Broil sweet potatoes until topping is melted and beginning to caramelize, 10 to 12 minutes. Transfer dish to wire rack and let cool for 10 minutes. Serve.

Sugar-glazed Walnuts

Servings: 6
Cooking Time: 5 Minutes

Ingredients:

- 1 Large egg white(s)
- 2 tablespoons Granulated white sugar
- ⅛ teaspoon Table salt
- 2 cups (7 ounces) Walnut halves

Directions:

1. Preheat the toaster oven to 400°F.

2. Use a whisk to beat the egg white(s) in a large bowl until quite foamy, more so than just well combined but certainly not yet a meringue.

3. If you're working with the quantities for a small batch, remove half of the foamy egg white.

4. If you're working with the quantities for a large batch, remove a quarter of it. It's fine to eyeball the amounts.

5. You can store the removed egg white in a sealed container to save for another use.

6. Stir in the sugar and salt. Add the walnut halves and toss to coat evenly and well, including the nuts' crevasses.

7. When the machine is at temperature, use a slotted spoon to transfer the walnut halves to the air fryer oven, taking care not to dislodge any coating. Gently spread the nuts into as close to one layer as you can. Air-fry undisturbed for 2 minutes.

8. Break up any clumps, toss the walnuts gently but well, and air-fry for 3 minutes more, tossing after 1 minute, then every 30 seconds thereafter, until the nuts are browned in spots and very aromatic. Watch carefully so they don't burn.

9. Gently dump the nuts onto a lipped baking sheet and spread them into one layer. Cool for at least 10 minutes before serving, separating any that stick together. The walnuts can be stored in a sealed container at room temperature for up to 5 days.

Buffalo Chicken Dip

Servings: 6

Cooking Time: 60 Minutes

Ingredients:

- 1 pound cream cheese
- ¾ cup Frank's RedHot Original Cayenne Pepper Sauce
- 3 cups shredded cooked chicken
- 1 cup ranch dressing
- 4 ounces blue cheese, crumbled (1 cup)
- 2 teaspoons Worcestershire sauce
- 4 ounces sharp cheddar cheese, shredded (1 cup)
- 2 scallions, sliced thin

Directions:

1. Adjust toaster oven rack to middle position and preheat the toaster oven to 350 degrees. Combine cream cheese and hot sauce in medium bowl and microwave until cream cheese is very soft, about 2 minutes, whisking halfway through microwaving. Whisk until smooth and no lumps of cream cheese remain. Stir in chicken, dressing, blue cheese, and Worcestershire until combined (visible bits of blue cheese are OK).

2. Transfer mixture to 2-quart baking dish and smooth top with rubber spatula. Bake for 20 minutes. Remove dish from toaster oven, stir dip, and sprinkle with cheddar. Return dish to oven and continue to bake until cheddar is melted and dip is bubbling around edges, 15 to 20 minutes longer. Transfer dish to wire rack and let cool for 10 minutes. Sprinkle with scallions and serve.

Roasted Green Beans With Goat Cheese And Hazelnuts

Servings: 2

Cooking Time: 45 Minutes

Ingredients:

- 12 ounces green beans, trimmed
- 3 tablespoons extra-virgin olive oil, divided
- ¼ teaspoon sugar
- ¼ teaspoon plus ⅛ teaspoon table salt, divided
- ¼ teaspoon plus ⅛ teaspoon pepper, divided
- 1 garlic clove, minced
- ½ teaspoon grated orange zest plus 1 teaspoon juice
- 1 teaspoon lemon juice
- ½ teaspoon Dijon mustard
- 1 tablespoon minced fresh chives
- 1 ounce goat cheese, crumbled (¼ cup)
- 2 tablespoons chopped toasted hazelnuts

Directions:

1. Adjust toaster oven rack to lowest position and preheat the toaster oven to 450 degrees. Toss green beans, 1 tablespoon oil, sugar, ¼ teaspoon salt, and ¼ teaspoon pepper together in bowl, then spread into even layer on small rimmed baking sheet.

2. Cover sheet tightly with aluminum foil and roast for 12 minutes. Remove foil and continue to roast until green beans are spotty brown, 10 to 15 minutes.

3. Meanwhile, combine garlic, orange zest, and remaining 2 tablespoons oil in large bowl and microwave until fragrant, 30 to 60 seconds; let steep for 1 minute. Whisk in orange juice, lemon juice, mustard, remaining ⅛ teaspoon salt, and remaining ⅛ teaspoon pepper. Add green beans and chives and toss to combine. Transfer to serving platter and sprinkle with goat cheese and hazelnuts. Serve.

Fried Apple Wedges

Servings: 4
Cooking Time: 9 Minutes

Ingredients:

- ¼ cup panko breadcrumbs
- ¼ cup pecans
- 1½ teaspoons cinnamon
- 1½ teaspoons brown sugar
- ¼ cup cornstarch
- 1 egg white
- 2 teaspoons water
- 1 medium apple
- oil for misting or cooking spray

Directions:

1. In a food processor, combine panko, pecans, cinnamon, and brown sugar. Process to make small crumbs.
2. Place cornstarch in a plastic bag or bowl with lid. In a shallow dish, beat together the egg white and water until slightly foamy.
3. Preheat the toaster oven to 390°F.
4. Cut apple into small wedges. The thickest edge should be no more than ⅜- to ½-inch thick. Cut away the core, but do not peel.
5. Place apple wedges in cornstarch, reseal bag or bowl, and shake to coat.
6. Dip wedges in egg wash, shake off excess, and roll in crumb mixture. Spray with oil.
7. Place apples in air fryer oven in single layer and air-fry for 5 minutes.Break apart any apples that have stuck together. Mist lightly with oil and cook 4 minutes longer, until crispy.

Cinnamon Apple Chips

Servings: 4
Cooking Time: 480 Minutes

Ingredients:

- 1 apple
- 1 tablespoon lemon juice
- ¼ teaspoon cinnamon

Directions:

1. Slice the apple into ⅛-inch-thick slices, preferably by using a mandoline slicer.
2. Place slices in a bowl of water mixed with the lemon juice to prevent browning. Remove after 2 minutes and dry thoroughly with paper towels.
3. Sprinkle the apple slices with cinnamon and place on the food tray.
4. Insert the food tray at mid position in the preheated oven.
5. Preheat the toaster oven to 130°F.
6. Remove when apple chips are crispy.

Crispy Tofu Bites

Servings: 4
Cooking Time: 20 Minutes

Ingredients:

- 1 pound Extra firm unflavored tofu
- Vegetable oil spray

Directions:

1. Wrap the piece of tofu in a triple layer of paper towels. Place it on a wooden cutting board and set a large pot on top of it to press out excess moisture. Set aside for 10 minutes.
2. Preheat the toaster oven to 400°F.
3. Remove the pot and unwrap the tofu. Cut it into 1-inch cubes. Place these in a bowl and coat them generously with vegetable oil spray. Toss gently, then spray generously again before tossing, until all are glistening.
4. Gently pour the tofu pieces into the air fryer oven, spread them into as close to one layer as possible, and air-fry for 20 minutes, using kitchen

tongs to gently rearrange the pieces at the 7- and 14-minute marks, until light brown and crisp.

5. Gently pour the tofu pieces onto a wire rack. Cool for 5 minutes before serving warm.

Bacon Bites

Servings: 6
Cooking Time: 20 Minutes

Ingredients:
- ½ cup packed dark brown sugar
- 6 slices bacon
- 6 very thin breadsticks from a 3-ounce package

Directions:
1. Preheat the toaster oven to 350°F. Line a 12 x 12-inch baking pan with aluminum foil.
2. Spread the brown sugar on a large plate. Wrap a bacon slice around each breadstick. Roll the bacon-wrapped breadstick in the brown sugar and press to adhere to the bacon. Place on the prepared pan.
3. Bake for 18 to 20 minutes, or until the bacon is cooked through. Immediately remove and place the warm sticks on wax paper (to prevent sticking). Let cool to room temperature before serving.

Pork Belly Scallion Yakitori

Servings: 3
Cooking Time: 10 Minutes

Ingredients:
- ¼ cup soy sauce
- 1 tablespoons sake
- 2 tablespoons mirin
- 2 teaspoons rice wine vinegar
- 2 tablespoons dark brown sugar
- ½ teaspoon onion powder
- ¼ teaspoon garlic powder
- ¼ teaspoon kosher salt
- 1½ inch piece of ginger, peeled and roughly sliced
- 1 pound of ½-inch thick sliced pork belly, cut into 2-inch pieces
- 6 scallions
- Lemon wedges, for serving

Directions:
1. Combine soy sauce, sake, mirin, rice wine vinegar, dark brown sugar, onion powder, garlic powder, kosher salt, and ginger in a bowl.
2. Add the pork belly to the marinade and massage the marinade into the meat.
3. Cover and place into the refrigerator for 5 hours.
4. Remove from the fridge and pat the pork belly dry with paper towels. Set aside and allow to sit at room temperature for 1 hour.
5. Cut off the thinner dark green part of the scallion and discard.
6. Cut the trimmed scallions into thirds.
7. Skewer a piece of pork belly, followed by a piece of scallion, then repeat until the skewer is filled. Place the skewers onto the food tray.
8. Preheat the toaster oven to 450°F.
9. Insert the food tray with yakitori at top position in the preheated oven.
10. Select the Broil and Shake functions, then press Start/Pause.
11. Flip the yakitori halfway through cooking. The Shake Reminder will let you know when.
12. Remove when done and serve with a wedge of lemon.

Avocado Egg Rolls

Servings: 8
Cooking Time: 8 Minutes

Ingredients:
- 8 full-size egg roll wrappers
- 1 medium avocado, sliced into 8 pieces
- 1 cup cooked black beans, divided
- ½ cup mild salsa, divided
- ½ cup shredded Mexican cheese, divided
- ⅓ cup filtered water, divided
- ½ cup sour cream
- 1 teaspoon chipotle hot sauce

Directions:
1. Preheat the toaster oven to 400°F.
2. Place the egg roll wrapper on a flat surface and place 1 strip of avocado down in the center.
3. Top the avocado with 2 tablespoons of black beans, 1 tablespoon of salsa, and 1 tablespoon of shredded cheese.
4. Place two of your fingers into the water, and then moisten the four outside edges of the egg roll wrapper with water (so the outer edges will secure shut).
5. Fold the bottom corner up, covering the filling. Then secure the sides over the top, remembering to lightly moisten them so they stick. Tightly roll the egg roll up and moisten the final flap of the wrapper and firmly press it into the egg roll to secure it shut.
6. Repeat Steps 2–5 until all 8 egg rolls are complete.
7. When ready to cook, spray the air fryer oven with olive oil spray and place the egg rolls into the air fryer oven. Depending on the size and type of air fryer oven you have, you may need to do this in two sets.
8. Air-fry for 4 minutes, flip, and then cook the remaining 4 minutes.
9. Repeat until all the egg rolls are cooked. Meanwhile, mix the sour cream with the hot sauce to serve as a dipping sauce.
10. Serve warm.

Grilled Ham & Muenster Cheese On Raisin Bread

Servings: 1
Cooking Time: 10 Minutes

Ingredients:
- 2 slices raisin bread
- 2 tablespoons butter, softened
- 2 teaspoons honey mustard
- 3 slices thinly sliced honey ham (about 3 ounces)
- 4 slices Muenster cheese (about 3 ounces)
- 2 toothpicks

Directions:
1. Preheat the toaster oven to 370°F.
2. Spread the softened butter on one side of both slices of raisin bread and place the bread, buttered side down on the counter. Spread the honey mustard on the other side of each slice of bread. Layer 2 slices of cheese, the ham and the remaining 2 slices of cheese on one slice of bread and top with the other slice of bread. Remember to leave the buttered side of the bread on the outside.
3. Transfer the sandwich to the air fryer oven and secure the sandwich with toothpicks.
4. Air-fry at 370°F for 5 minutes. Flip the sandwich over, remove the toothpicks and air-fry for another 5 minutes. Cut the sandwich in half and enjoy!!

Beef Satay With Peanut Dipping Sauce

Servings: 4

Cooking Time: 60 Minutes

Ingredients:

- SKEWERS
- 1 pound flank steak, trimmed
- 2 tablespoons soy sauce
- 2 tablespoons vegetable oil
- 2 tablespoons packed dark brown sugar
- 2 tablespoons minced fresh cilantro
- 2 scallions, sliced thin
- 1½ tablespoons ketchup
- 1 garlic clove, minced
- ½ teaspoon sriracha
- SPICY PEANUT DIPPING SAUCE
- ¼ cup peanut butter (creamy or chunky)
- 2 tablespoons hot water, plus extra as needed
- 1½ tablespoons lime juice
- 1 scallion, sliced thin
- 1 tablespoon ketchup
- 1½ teaspoons soy sauce
- 1½ teaspoons packed dark brown sugar
- 1½ teaspoons minced fresh cilantro
- ¾ teaspoon sriracha
- 1 garlic clove, minced

Directions:

1. FOR THE SKEWERS: Slice beef against grain ¼ inch thick (you should have at least 20 slices).

2. Combine soy sauce, oil, sugar, cilantro, scallions, ketchup, garlic, and sriracha in medium bowl; add beef; and toss to combine. Cover and refrigerate for 15 minutes. Weave 1 beef slice evenly onto each skewer, leaving at least 1 inch at bottom of skewer exposed (Skewers can be refrigerated for up to 24 hours.)

3. FOR THE SPICY PEANUT DIPPING SAUCE: Whisk peanut butter and hot water together in medium bowl. Stir in lime juice, scallion, ketchup, soy sauce, sugar, cilantro, sriracha, and garlic. Adjust consistency with extra hot water as needed; set aside for serving.

4. Adjust toaster oven rack to middle position, select broiler function, and heat broiler. Set small wire rack in aluminum foil–lined small rimmed baking sheet and spray rack with vegetable oil spray. Arrange skewers in two rows across width of prepared rack with all exposed skewer ends facing center of rack. Cover skewer ends in center of sheet with strip of foil and secure by crimping tightly at edges. Broil skewers until beef is no longer pink on top, 2 to 3 minutes. Flip skewers and continue to broil until beef is fully cooked and spotty brown, 4 to 6 minutes. Serve with peanut sauce.

All-purpose Cornbread

Servings: 6

Cooking Time: 60 Minutes

Ingredients:

- 1½ cups (7½ ounces) all-purpose flour
- 1 cup (5 ounces) cornmeal
- 2 teaspoons baking powder
- ¼ teaspoon baking soda
- ¾ teaspoon table salt
- ¼ cup packed (1¾ ounces) light brown sugar
- ¾ cup frozen corn, thawed
- 1 cup buttermilk
- 2 large eggs
- 8 tablespoons unsalted butter, melted and cooled

Directions:

1. Adjust toaster oven rack to middle position and preheat the toaster oven to 400 degrees. Spray 8-inch square baking dish or pan with vegetable oil spray. Whisk flour, cornmeal, baking powder, baking soda, and salt together in medium bowl; set aside.

2. Process sugar, corn, and buttermilk in food processor until combined, about 5 seconds. Add eggs and process until well combined (corn lumps will remain), about 5 seconds.

3. Using rubber spatula, make well in center of dry ingredients; pour wet ingredients into well. Begin folding dry ingredients into wet, giving mixture only a few turns to barely combine. Add melted butter and continue to fold until dry ingredients are just moistened. Transfer batter to prepared dish and smooth top.

4. Bake until deep golden brown and toothpick inserted in center comes out clean, 25 to 35 minutes. Let cornbread cool in dish on wire rack for 10 minutes. Remove bread from dish and let cool until just warm, about 10 minutes longer. Serve. (Cornbread can be wrapped in aluminum foil and reheated in 350-degree oven for 10 to 15 minutes.)

Ham And Cheese Palmiers

Servings: 30

Cooking Time: 60 Minutes

Ingredients:

- 1 (9½ by 9-inch) sheet puff pastry, thawed
- 2 tablespoons Dijon mustard
- 2 teaspoons minced fresh thyme
- 2 ounces Parmesan cheese, grated (1 cup)
- 4 ounces thinly sliced deli ham

Directions:

1. Roll puff pastry into 12-inch square on lightly floured counter. Brush evenly with mustard; sprinkle with thyme and Parmesan; pressing gently to adhere, and lay ham evenly over top. Roll up opposite sides of pastry until they meet in middle. Wrap pastry log in plastic wrap and refrigerate until firm, about 1 hour.

2. Adjust toaster oven rack to middle position, select air-fry or convection setting, and preheat the toaster oven to 400 degrees. Line large and small rimmed baking sheets with parchment paper. Using sharp knife, trim ends of log, then slice into ⅓-inch-thick pieces. Space desired number of palmiers at least 1 inch apart on prepared small sheet; space remaining palmiers evenly on prepared large sheet. Re-shape palmiers as needed.

3. Bake small sheet of palmiers until golden brown and crisp, 15 to 25 minutes. Transfer palmiers to wire rack and let cool for 15 minutes before serving. (Palmiers can be held at room temperature for up to 6 hours before serving.)

4. Freeze remaining large sheet of palmiers until firm, about 1 hour. Transfer palmiers to 1-gallon zipper-lock bag and freeze for up to 1 month. Cook frozen palmiers as directed; do not thaw.

Sesame Green Beans

Servings: 4

Cooking Time: 8 Minutes

Ingredients:

- 1 pound green beans, stems trimmed
- 1 tablespoon olive oil
- 1 teaspoon sesame oil
- 1 tablespoon sesame seeds
- Pinch sea salt

Directions:

1. Preheat the toaster oven to 350°F on AIR FRY for 5 minutes.

2. In a large bowl, toss the green beans, olive oil, and sesame oil.

3. Place the air-fryer basket in the baking tray and spread the beans in the basket.

4. Place the tray in position 2 and air fry for 8 minutes, shaking the basket at the halfway point. The beans should be lightly golden and fragrant.

5. Transfer the beans to a serving plate and serve topped with the sesame seeds and seasoned with salt.

Smoked Gouda Bacon Macaroni And Cheese

Servings: 10-12
Cooking Time: 30 Minutes

Ingredients:

- 1 (4 oz.) French baguette, torn
- 6 slices cooked bacon, chopped
- 1/4 cup loosely packed parsley
- 2 Tablespoons butter, melted
- 1 package (16 oz.) corkscrew or elbow pasta
- 1/3 cup butter
- 1/4 cup flour
- 4 cups milk
- 1 package (8 oz.) extra sharp Cheddar cheese, shredded
- 1 package (8 oz.) smoked Gouda cheese, shredded
- 2 1/2 teaspoons Creole seasoning

Directions:

1. Preheat the toaster oven to 400°F.

2. Using S-blade with food processor running, drop bread, 1/2 of the bacon and parsley into food chute. Process until finely chopped.

Gradually add melted butter; process until crumbs form. Set aside.

3. Cook pasta according to package directions for al dente. Drain and rinse with cold water. Set aside.

4. Melt 1/3 cup butter in Dutch oven over medium-high heat. Gradually add flour, whisking until smooth, about 1 minute. Slowly add milk, stirring 8 to 10 minutes until mixture is thickened and smooth. Remove from heat.

5. Stir in cheeses, remaining bacon and Creole seasoning until cheese is melted. Fold in pasta.

6. Pour mixture into 11x7-inch baking dish sprayed with nonstick cooking spray. Sprinkle with breadcrumb mixture.

7. Bake 25 to 30 minutes or until crumbs are browned and mixture is heated through.

Fiery Bacon-wrapped Dates

Servings: 16
Cooking Time: 6 Minutes

Ingredients:

- 8 Thin-cut bacon strips, halved widthwise (gluten-free, if a concern)
- 16 Medium or large Medjool dates, pitted
- 3 tablespoons (about ¾ ounce) Shredded semi-firm mozzarella
- 32 Pickled jalapeño rings

Directions:

1. Preheat the toaster oven to 400°F.

2. Lay a bacon strip half on a clean, dry work surface. Split one date lengthwise without cutting through it, so that it opens like a pocket. Set it on one end of the bacon strip and open it a bit. Place 1 teaspoon of the shredded cheese and 2 pickled jalapeño rings in the date, then gently squeeze it together without fully closing it (just to hold the

stuffing inside). Roll up the date in the bacon strip and set it bacon seam side down on a cutting board. Repeat this process with the remaining bacon strip halves, dates, cheese, and jalapeño rings.

3. Place the bacon-wrapped dates bacon seam side down in the air fryer oven. Air-fry undisturbed for 6 minutes, or until crisp and brown.

4. Use kitchen tongs to gently transfer the wrapped dates to a wire rack or serving platter. Cool for a few minutes before serving.

VEGETABLES AND VEGETARIAN

Roasted Fennel Salad

Servings: 3
Cooking Time: 20 Minutes

Ingredients:

- 3 cups (about ¾ pound) Trimmed fennel, roughly chopped
- 1½ tablespoons Olive oil
- ¼ teaspoon Table salt
- ¼ teaspoon Ground black pepper
- 1½ tablespoons White balsamic vinegar

Directions:

1. Preheat the toaster oven to 400°F.
2. Toss the fennel, olive oil, salt, and pepper in a large bowl until the fennel is well coated in the oil.
3. When the machine is at temperature, pour the fennel into the air fryer oven, spreading it out into as close to one layer as possible. Air-fry for 20 minutes, tossing and rearranging the fennel pieces twice so that any covered or touching parts get exposed to the air currents, until golden at the edges and softened.
4. Pour the fennel into a serving bowl. Add the vinegar while hot. Toss well, then cool a couple of minutes before serving. Or serve at room temperature.

Onions

Servings: 4
Cooking Time: 18 Minutes

Ingredients:

- 2 yellow onions (Vidalia or 1015 recommended)
- salt and pepper
- ¼ teaspoon ground thyme
- ¼ teaspoon smoked paprika
- 2 teaspoons olive oil
- 1 ounce Gruyère cheese, grated

Directions:

1. Peel onions and halve lengthwise (vertically).
2. Sprinkle cut sides of onions with salt, pepper, thyme, and paprika.
3. Place each onion half, cut-surface up, on a large square of aluminum foil. Pull sides of foil up to cup around onion. Drizzle cut surface of onions with oil.
4. Crimp foil at top to seal closed.
5. Place wrapped onions in air fryer oven and air-fry at 390°F for 18 minutes. When done, onions should be soft enough to pierce with fork but still slightly firm.
6. Open foil just enough to sprinkle each onion with grated cheese.
7. Air-fry for 30 seconds to 1 minute to melt cheese.

Roasted Garlic

Servings: 1
Cooking Time: 20 Minutes

Ingredients:

- 3 whole garlic buds
- 3 tablespoons olive oil
- Salt and freshly ground black pepper

Directions:

1. Preheat the toaster oven to 450° F.
2. Place the garlic buds in an oiled or nonstick 8½ × 8½ × 2-inch square baking (cake) pan.
3. BAKE, uncovered, for 20 minutes, or until the buds are tender when pierced with a skewer or sharp knife. When cool enough to handle, peel and mash the baked cloves with a fork into the olive oil. Season with salt and pepper to taste.

Mushrooms

Servings: 4

Cooking Time: 12 Minutes

Ingredients:

- 8 ounces whole white button mushrooms
- ½ teaspoon salt
- ⅛ teaspoon pepper
- ¼ teaspoon garlic powder
- ¼ teaspoon onion powder
- 5 tablespoons potato starch
- 1 egg, beaten
- ¾ cup panko breadcrumbs
- oil for misting or cooking spray

Directions:

1. Place mushrooms in a large bowl. Add the salt, pepper, garlic and onion powders, and stir well to distribute seasonings.

2. Add potato starch to mushrooms and toss in bowl until well coated.

3. Dip mushrooms in beaten egg, roll in panko crumbs, and mist with oil or cooking spray.

4. Place mushrooms in air fryer oven. You can cook them all at once, and it's okay if a few are stacked.

5. Air-fry at 390°F for 5 minutes. Rotate, then continue cooking for 7 more minutes, until golden brown and crispy.

Crunchy Roasted Potatoes

Servings: 5

Cooking Time: 25 Minutes

Ingredients:

- 2 pounds Small (1- to 1½-inch-diameter) red, white, or purple potatoes
- 2 tablespoons Olive oil
- 2 teaspoons Table salt
- ¾ teaspoon Garlic powder
- ½ teaspoon Ground black pepper

Directions:

1. Preheat the toaster oven to 400°F.

2. Toss the potatoes, oil, salt, garlic powder, and pepper in a large bowl until the spuds are evenly and thoroughly coated.

3. When the machine is at temperature, pour the potatoes into the air fryer oven, spreading them into an even layer (although they may be stacked on top of each other). Air-fry for 25 minutes, tossing twice, until the potatoes are tender but crunchy.

4. Pour the contents of the air fryer oven into a serving bowl. Cool for 5 minutes before serving.

Roasted Eggplant Halves With Herbed Ricotta

Servings: 3

Cooking Time: 20 Minutes

Ingredients:

- 3 5- to 6-ounce small eggplants, stemmed
- Olive oil spray
- ¼ teaspoon Table salt
- ¼ teaspoon Ground black pepper
- ½ cup Regular or low-fat ricotta
- 1½ tablespoons Minced fresh basil leaves
- 1¼ teaspoons Minced fresh oregano leaves
- Honey

Directions:

1. Preheat the toaster oven to 325°F (or 330°F, if that's the closest setting).

2. Cut the eggplants in half lengthwise. Set them cut side up on your work surface. Using the tip of a paring knife, make a series of slits about three-quarters down into the flesh of each

eggplant half; work at a 45-degree angle to the (former) stem across the vegetable and make the slits about ½ inch apart. Make a second set of equidistant slits at a 90-degree angle to the first slits, thus creating a crosshatch pattern in the vegetable.

3. Generously coat the cut sides of the eggplants with olive oil spray. Sprinkle the salt and pepper over the cut surfaces.

4. Set the eggplant halves cut side up in the air fryer oven with as much air space between them as possible. Air-fry undisturbed for 20 minutes, or until soft and golden.

5. Use kitchen tongs to gently transfer the eggplant halves to serving plates or a platter. Cool for 5 minutes.

6. Whisk the ricotta, basil, and oregano in a small bowl until well combined. Top the eggplant halves with this mixture. Drizzle the halves with honey to taste before serving warm.

Pimiento-and-olive Stuffed Potatoes

Servings: 2
Cooking Time: 8 Minutes

Ingredients:

- 2 large baking potatoes, baked
- Stuffing:
- 3 tablespoons minced pimientos
- 3 tablespoons pitted and chopped black olives
- 3 tablespoons nonfat sour cream
- 1 teaspoon paprika
- Salt and butcher's pepper to taste

Directions:

1. Scoop out the pulp of the baked potatoes and place in a bowl.

2. Add the stuffing ingredients, blending well, and fill the potato shells. Place the potatoes on a broiling rack with a pan underneath.

3. BROIL for 8 minutes, or until the top is lightly browned.

Golden Grilled Cheese Tomato Sandwich

Servings: 2
Cooking Time: 10 Minutes

Ingredients:

- 4 slices whole-grain bread
- 4 teaspoons salted butter at room temperature, divided
- 4 to 6 slices cheddar cheese, or your favorite cheese
- 1 large tomato, thinly sliced

Directions:

1. Preheat the toaster oven to 350°F on AIR FRY for 5 minutes.

2. Place the air-fryer basket in the baking sheet and set aside.

3. Butter all four pieces of bread, using 1 teaspoon of butter for each and place 2 pieces of bread, butter-side down, in the basket. Evenly divide the cheese between the 2 bread slices and top with tomato slices. Place the remaining 2 pieces of bread on the tomatoes, butter-side up.

4. Place the tray in position 2 and air fry for 5 minutes until golden brown. Flip the sandwiches and air fry until the cheese is melted and the other side of the bread is golden brown, about 5 minutes. Serve.

Perfect Asparagus

Servings: 3
Cooking Time: 10 Minutes

Ingredients:

- 1 pound Very thin asparagus spears
- 2 tablespoons Olive oil
- 1 teaspoon Coarse sea salt or kosher salt
- ¾ teaspoon Finely grated lemon zest

Directions:

1. Preheat the toaster oven to 400°F.
2. Trim just enough off the bottom of the asparagus spears so they'll fit in the air fryer oven. Put the spears on a large plate and drizzle them with some of the olive oil. Turn them over and drizzle more olive oil, working to get all the spears coated.
3. When the machine is at temperature, place the spears in one direction in the air fryer oven. They may be touching. Air-fry for 10 minutes, tossing and rearranging the spears twice, until tender.
4. Dump the contents of the air fryer oven on a serving platter. Spread out the spears. Sprinkle them with the salt and lemon zest while still warm. Serve at once.

Moroccan Cauliflower

Servings: 6
Cooking Time: 15 Minutes

Ingredients:

- 1 tablespoon curry powder
- 2 teaspoons smoky paprika
- ½ teaspoon ground cumin
- ½ teaspoon salt
- 1 head cauliflower, cut into bite-size pieces
- ¼ cup red wine vinegar
- 2 tablespoons extra-virgin olive oil
- 2 tablespoons chopped parsley

Directions:

1. Preheat the toaster oven to 370°F.
2. In a large bowl, mix the curry powder, paprika, cumin, and salt. Add the cauliflower and stir to coat. Pour the red wine vinegar over the top and continue stirring.
3. Place the cauliflower into the air fryer oven; drizzle olive oil over the top.
4. Cook the cauliflower for 5 minutes, toss, and cook another 5 minutes. Raise the temperature to 400°F and continue cooking for 4 to 6 minutes, or until crispy.

Lentil-stuffed Zucchini

Servings: 2
Cooking Time: 50 Minutes

Ingredients:

- 2 large zucchini
- 2 teaspoons olive oil
- 1 (15-ounce) can low-sodium lentils, drained and rinsed
- 1 large tomato, chopped
- 1 scallion, both white and green parts, chopped
- ½ jalapeño pepper, minced
- ½ cup corn kernels, fresh or frozen (thawed)
- 1 tablespoon fresh cilantro, chopped
- 1 teaspoon minced garlic
- 1 teaspoon ground cumin
- ¼ teaspoon chili powder
- ½ cup shredded Monterey Jack cheese

Directions:

1. Preheat the toaster oven to 400°F on BAKE for 5 minutes.
2. Line the baking tray with parchment paper.

3. Cut the zucchini in half lengthwise and scoop out the insides so that you have a hollow shell (about ¼-inch thick all the way around).

4. Lightly oil both sides of the zucchini shells and set them on the baking sheet.

5. In a large bowl, stir the lentils, tomato, scallion, jalapeño, corn, cilantro, garlic, cumin, and chili powder until well mixed.

6. Spoon the lentil mixture into the zucchini and top with the cheese.

7. Bake for 50 minutes. The zucchini should be tender, the filling heated through, and the cheese melted and lightly browned. Serve.

Baked Mac And Cheese

Servings: 4
Cooking Time: 45 Minutes

Ingredients:
- Oil spray (hand-pumped)
- 1½ cups whole milk, room temperature
- ½ cup heavy (whipping) cream, room temperature
- 1 cup shredded cheddar cheese
- 4 ounces cream cheese, room temperature
- ½ teaspoon dry mustard
- ⅛ teaspoon sea salt
- ⅛ teaspoon freshly ground black pepper
- 1¼ cups dried elbow macaroni
- ¼ cup bread crumbs
- 2 tablespoons grated Parmesan cheese
- 1 tablespoon salted butter, melted

Directions:
1. Place the rack in position 1 and preheat the toaster oven to 375°F on CONVECTION BAKE for 5 minutes.

2. Lightly coat an 8-inch-square baking dish with the oil spray.

3. In a large bowl, stir the milk, cream, cheddar, cream cheese, mustard, salt, and pepper until well combined.

4. Transfer the mixture to the baking dish, stir in the macaroni and cover tightly with foil.

5. Bake for 35 minutes.

6. While the macaroni is baking, in a small bowl, stir the bread crumbs, Parmesan, and butter to form coarse crumbs. Set aside.

7. Take the baking dish out of the oven, uncover, stir, and evenly cover with the bread crumb mixture.

8. Bake uncovered for an additional 10 minutes until the pasta is tender, bubbly, and golden brown. Serve.

Yellow Squash

Servings: 4
Cooking Time: 10 Minutes

Ingredients:
- 1 large yellow squash (about 1½ cups)
- 2 eggs
- ¼ cup buttermilk
- 1 cup panko breadcrumbs
- ¼ cup white cornmeal
- ½ teaspoon salt
- oil for misting or cooking spray

Directions:
1. Preheat the toaster oven to 390°F.

2. Cut the squash into ¼-inch slices.

3. In a shallow dish, beat together eggs and buttermilk.

4. In sealable plastic bag or container with lid, combine ¼ cup panko crumbs, white cornmeal, and salt. Shake to mix well.

5. Place the remaining ¾ cup panko crumbs in a separate shallow dish.

6. Dump all the squash slices into the egg/buttermilk mixture. Stir to coat.

7. Remove squash from buttermilk mixture with a slotted spoon, letting excess drip off, and transfer to the panko/cornmeal mixture. Close bag or container and shake well to coat.

8. Remove squash from crumb mixture, letting excess fall off. Return squash to egg/buttermilk mixture, stirring gently to coat. If you need more liquid to coat all the squash, add a little more buttermilk.

9. Remove each squash slice from egg wash and dip in a dish of ¾ cup panko crumbs.

10. Mist squash slices with oil or cooking spray and place in air fryer oven. Squash should be in a single layer, but it's okay if the slices crowd together and overlap a little.

11. Air-fry at 390°F for 5 minutes. Break up any that have stuck together. Mist again with oil or spray.

12. Cook 5 minutes longer and check. If necessary, mist again with oil and cook an additional two minutes, until squash slices are golden brown and crisp.

Home Fries

Servings: 4
Cooking Time: 20 Minutes

Ingredients:
- 3 pounds potatoes, cut into 1-inch cubes
- ½ teaspoon oil
- salt and pepper

Directions:
1. In a large bowl, mix the potatoes and oil thoroughly.
2. Air-fry at 390°F for 10 minutes and redistribute potatoes.

3. Air-fry for an additional 10 minutes, until brown and crisp.

4. Season with salt and pepper to taste.

Roasted Corn Salad

Servings: 3
Cooking Time: 15 Minutes

Ingredients:
- 3 4-inch lengths husked and de-silked corn on the cob
- Olive oil spray
- 1 cup Packed baby arugula leaves
- 12 Cherry tomatoes, halved
- Up to 3 Medium scallion(s), trimmed and thinly sliced
- 2 tablespoons Lemon juice
- 1 tablespoon Olive oil
- 1½ teaspoons Honey
- ¼ teaspoon Mild paprika
- ¼ teaspoon Dried oregano
- ¼ teaspoon, plus more to taste Table salt
- ¼ teaspoon Ground black pepper

Directions:
1. Preheat the toaster oven to 400°F.
2. When the machine is at temperature, lightly coat the pieces of corn on the cob with olive oil spray. Set the pieces of corn in the air fryer oven with as much air space between them as possible. Air-fry undisturbed for 15 minutes, or until the corn is charred in a few spots.
3. Use kitchen tongs to transfer the corn to a wire rack. Cool for 15 minutes.
4. Cut the kernels off the ears by cutting the fat end off each piece so it will stand up straight on a cutting board, then running a knife down the corn. (Or you can save your fingers and buy a fancy tool to remove kernels from corn cobs.

Check it out at online kitchenware stores.) Scoop the kernels into a serving bowl.

5. Chop the arugula into bite-size bits and add these to the kernels. Add the tomatoes and scallions, too. Whisk the lemon juice, olive oil, honey, paprika, oregano, salt, and pepper in a small bowl until the honey dissolves. Pour over the salad and toss well to coat, tasting for extra salt before serving.

Roasted Veggie Kebabs

Servings: 4
Cooking Time: 45 Minutes

Ingredients:

- Brushing mixture:
- 3 tablespoons olive oil
- 1 tablespoon soy sauce
- 1 teaspoon garlic powder
- 1 teaspoon ground cumin
- 2 tablespoons balsamic vinegar
- Salt and freshly ground black pepper to taste
- Cauliflower, zucchini, onion, broccoli, bell pepper, mushrooms, celery, cabbage, beets, and the like, cut into approximately 2 × 2-inch pieces

Directions:

1. Preheat the toaster oven to 400° F.
2. Combine the brushing mixture ingredients in a small bowl, mixing well. Set aside.
3. Skewer the vegetable pieces on 4 9-inch metal skewers and place the skewers lengthwise on a broiling rack with a pan underneath.
4. BAKE for 40 minutes, or until the vegetables are tender, brushing with the mixture every 10 minutes.
5. BROIL for 5 minutes, or until lightly browned.

Cheesy Texas Toast

Servings: 2
Cooking Time: 4 Minutes

Ingredients:

- 2 1-inch-thick slice(s) Italian bread (each about 4 inches across)
- 4 teaspoons Softened butter
- 2 teaspoons Minced garlic
- ¼ cup (about ¾ ounce) Finely grated Parmesan cheese

Directions:

1. Preheat the toaster oven to 400°F.
2. Spread one side of a slice of bread with 2 teaspoons butter. Sprinkle with 1 teaspoon minced garlic, followed by 2 tablespoons grated cheese. Repeat this process if you're making one or more additional toasts.
3. When the machine is at temperature, put the bread slice(s) cheese side up in the air fryer oven (with as much air space between them as possible if you're making more than one). Air-fry undisturbed for 4 minutes, or until browned and crunchy.
4. Use a nonstick-safe spatula to transfer the toasts cheese side up to a wire rack. Cool for 5 minutes before serving.

Pecan Parmesan Cauliflower

Servings: 4
Cooking Time: 35 Minutes

Ingredients:

- 2½ cups (frozen thawed or fresh) thinly sliced cauliflower florets
- Salt and freshly ground black pepper
- 3 tablespoons freshly grated Parmesan cheese
- ½ cup ground pecans

Directions:

1. Preheat the toaster oven to 400° F.

2. Combine the florets and oil in a 1-quart 8½ × 8½ × 4-inch ovenproof baking dish, tossing to coat well. Season to taste with salt and pepper. Cover the dish with aluminum foil.

3. BAKE for 25 minutes, or until tender. Uncover and sprinkle with the cheese and pecans.

4. BROIL for 10 minutes, or until lightly browned.

Classic Stuffed Baked Potatoes

Servings: 4

Cooking Time: 58 Minutes

Ingredients:

- 2 large baking potatoes, slit on top with a knife
- ⅛ teaspoon paprika
- Salt and freshly ground black pepper to taste
- Stuffing:
- 1 teaspoon margarine
- 1 egg, lightly beaten
- ½ cup nonfat sour cream
- 4 tablespoons fresh or frozen and thawed chives

Directions:

1. Preheat the toaster oven to 400° F.

2. BAKE the potatoes on the oven rack for 50 minutes, or until tender. Open the slits with a knife and scoop out the pulp with a teaspoon. Set the potato shells aside.

3. Combine the stuffing ingredients and add the pulp, mixing well, until light and fluffy. Refill the potato shells.

4. BROIL 8 minutes, or until the top is lightly browned. Sprinkle with the chives before serving.

Almond-crusted Spinach Soufflé

Servings: 4

Cooking Time: 25 Minutes

Ingredients:

- 2 tablespoons reduced-fat sour cream
- 1 tablespoon unbleached flour
- 2 cups fresh spinach, rinsed well, drained, and finely chopped, or 1 10-oz. package frozen spinach, thawed, drained, and blotted dry
- 1 egg, separated
- 1 teaspoon olive oil
- Salt and freshly ground black pepper
- Grated nutmeg
- ¼ cup finely chopped almonds

Directions:

1. Preheat the toaster oven to 350° F.

2. Stir together the sour cream and flour in a medium bowl until smooth. Add the spinach, egg yolk, and oil, mixing well and seasoning to taste with the salt, pepper, and nutmeg.

3. Beat the egg white until stiff and fold into the spinach mixture. Pour into a 1-quart 8½ × 8½ × 4-inch ovenproof baking dish. Sprinkle with the almonds.

4. BAKE, uncovered, for 25 minutes, or until firm and the topping is lightly browned.

Eggplant And Tomato Slices

Servings: 4

Cooking Time: 36 Minutes

Ingredients:

- 2 tablespoons olive oil
- ¼ teaspoon garlic powder
- 4 ½-inch-thick slices eggplant
- 4 ¼-inch-thick slices fresh tomato
- 2 tablespoons tomato sauce or salsa

- ½ cup shredded Parmesan cheese
- Salt and freshly ground black pepper to taste
- 2 tablespoons chopped fresh basil, cilantro, parsley, or oregano

Directions:

1. Whisk together the oil and garlic powder in a small bowl. Brush each eggplant slice with the mixture and place in an oiled or nonstick 8½ × 8½ × 2-inch square baking (cake) pan.

2. BROIL for 20 minutes. Remove the pan from the oven and turn the pieces with tongs. Top each with a slice of tomato and broil another 10 minutes, or until tender. Remove the pan from the oven, brush each slice with tomato sauce or salsa, and sprinkle generously with Parmesan cheese. Season to taste with salt and pepper. Broil again for 6 minutes, until the tops are browned.

3. Garnish with the fresh herb and serve.

Salmon Salad With Steamboat Dressing

Servings: 4
Cooking Time: 18 Minutes

Ingredients:

- ¼ teaspoon salt
- 1½ teaspoons dried dill weed
- 1 tablespoon fresh lemon juice
- 8 ounces fresh or frozen salmon fillet (skin on)
- 8 cups shredded romaine, Boston, or other leaf lettuce
- 8 spears cooked asparagus, cut in 1-inch pieces
- 8 cherry tomatoes, halved or quartered

Directions:

1. Mix the salt and dill weed together. Rub the lemon juice over the salmon on both sides and sprinkle the dill and salt all over. Refrigerate for 15 to 20 minutes.

2. Make Steamboat Dressing and refrigerate while cooking salmon and preparing salad.

3. Cook salmon in air fryer oven at 330°F for 18 minutes. Cooking time will vary depending on thickness of fillets. When done, salmon should flake with fork but still be moist and tender.

4. Remove salmon from air fryer oven and cool slightly. At this point, the skin should slide off easily. Cut salmon into 4 pieces and discard skin.

5. Divide the lettuce among 4 plates. Scatter asparagus spears and tomato pieces evenly over the lettuce, allowing roughly 2 whole spears and 2 whole cherry tomatoes per plate.

6. Top each salad with one portion of the salmon and drizzle with a tablespoon of dressing. Serve with additional dressing to pass at the table.

Ranch Potatoes

Servings: 2
Cooking Time: 50 Minutes

Ingredients:

- 2 medium russet potatoes, scrubbed and cut lengthwise into ¼-inch strips
- 1 medium onion, chopped
- 2 tablespoons vegetable oil
- 2 tablespoons barbecue sauce
- ¼ teaspoon hot sauce
- Salt and freshly ground black pepper

Directions:

1. Preheat the toaster oven to 400° F.

2. Combine all the ingredients in a medium bowl, mixing well and adjusting the seasonings to taste.

3. Place equal portions of the potatoes on two 12 × 12-inch squares of heavy-duty aluminum foil.

Fold up the edges of the foil to form a sealed packet and place on the oven rack.

4. BAKE for 40 minutes, or until the potatoes are tender. Carefully open the packet and fold back the foil.

5. BROIL 10 minutes, or until the potatoes are browned.

Grits Casserole

Servings: 4

Cooking Time: 30 Minutes

Ingredients:

- 10 fresh asparagus spears, cut into 1-inch pieces
- 2 cups cooked grits, cooled to room temperature
- 1 egg, beaten
- 2 teaspoons Worcestershire sauce
- ½ teaspoon garlic powder
- ¼ teaspoon salt
- 2 slices provolone cheese (about 1½ ounces)
- oil for misting or cooking spray

Directions:

1. Mist asparagus spears with oil and air-fry at 390°F for 5 minutes, until crisp-tender.

2. In a medium bowl, mix together the grits, egg, Worcestershire, garlic powder, and salt.

3. Spoon half of grits mixture into air fryer oven baking pan and top with asparagus.

4. Tear cheese slices into pieces and layer evenly on top of asparagus.

5. Top with remaining grits.

6. Bake at 360°F for 25 minutes. The casserole will rise a little as it cooks. When done, the top will have browned lightly with just a hint of crispiness.

Potatoes Au Gratin

Servings: 4

Cooking Time: 40 Minutes

Ingredients:

- Mixture:
- ½ cup fat-free half-and-half
- ¼ cup nonfat plain yogurt
- 2 tablespoons margarine
- 2 tablespoons unbleached flour
- 1 teaspoon garlic powder
- ¼ cup shredded low-fat mozzarella cheese
- 2 tablespoons grated Parmesan cheese
- Salt and butcher's pepper to taste
- 2 cups peeled and diced potatoes
- ½ cup chopped onion
- 1 tablespoon fresh or frozen chives
- ¼ teaspoon paprika

Directions:

1. Preheat the toaster oven to 400° F.

2. Process the mixture ingredients in a food processor or blender until smooth. Pour into a 1-quart 8½ × 8½ × 4-inch ovenproof baking dish.

3. Add the potatoes, onion, chives, and paprika and stir to mix well. Cover the dish with aluminum foil.

4. BAKE, covered, for 40 minutes, or until the potatoes and onion are tender.

Brussels Sprout And Ham Salad

Servings: 3

Cooking Time: 12 Minutes

Ingredients:

- 1 pound 2-inch-in-length Brussels sprouts, quartered through the stem
- 6 ounces Smoked ham steak, any rind removed, diced (gluten-free, if a concern)

- ¼ teaspoon Caraway seeds
- Vegetable oil spray
- ¼ cup Brine from a jar of pickles (gluten-free, if a concern)
- ¾ teaspoon Ground black pepper

Directions:

1. Preheat the toaster oven to 375°F .

2. Toss the Brussels sprout quarters, ham, and caraway seeds in a bowl until well combined. Generously coat the top of the mixture with vegetable oil spray, toss again, spray again, and repeat a couple of times until the vegetables and ham are glistening.

3. When the machine is at temperature, scrape the contents of the bowl into the air fryer oven, spreading it into as close to one layer as you can. Air-fry for 12 minutes, tossing and rearranging the pieces at least twice so that any covered or touching parts are eventually exposed to the air currents, until the Brussels sprouts are tender and a little brown at the edges.

4. Dump the contents of the air fryer oven into a serving bowl. Scrape any caraway seeds from the bottom of the air fryer oven or the tray under the pan attachment into the bowl as well. Add the pickle brine and pepper. Toss well to coat. Serve warm.

Crisp Cajun Potato Wedges

Servings: 2
Cooking Time: 70 Minutes

Ingredients:

- 2 medium baking potatoes, scrubbed, halved, and cut lengthwise into ½-inch-wide wedges
- 1 tablespoon vegetable oil
- Cajun seasonings:
- ¼ teaspoon chili powder
- ⅛ teaspoon cayenne
- ⅛ teaspoon dry mustard
- ⅛ teaspoon salt
- ⅛ teaspoon cumin
- ¼ teaspoon onion powder
- ¼ teaspoon paprika

Directions:

1. Preheat the toaster oven to 450° F.

2. Soak the potato wedges in cold water for 10 minutes to crisp. Drain on paper towels. Brush with the oil.

3. Combine the Cajun seasonings in a small bowl, add the wedges, and toss to coat well. Transfer to an oiled or nonstick 8½ × 8½ × 2-inch square baking (cake) pan.

4. BAKE, covered, for 40 minutes, or until the potatoes are tender. Carefully remove the cover.

5. BROIL for 20 minutes to crisp, turning with a tongs every 5 minutes until the desired crispness is achieved.

Balsamic Sweet Potatoes

Servings: 4
Cooking Time: 40 Minutes

Ingredients:

- 2 medium sweet potatoes, scrubbed (or peeled) and sliced into 1-inch rounds
- 3 tablespoons olive oil
- 2 tablespoons balsamic vinegar
- 2 teaspoons molasses
- ½ teaspoon garlic powder
- Salt and freshly ground black pepper to taste
- 1 tablespoon grated lemon zest

Directions:

1. Preheat the toaster oven to 400° F.
2. Mix the potatoes, oil, balsamic vinegar, molasses, and garlic powder together in an oiled or nonstick 8½ × 8½ × 2-inch square baking (cake) pan. Cover the pan with aluminum foil.
3. BAKE, covered, for 30 minutes, or until tender. Remove the cover.
4. BROIL for 10 minutes, or until the potatoes are lightly browned. Season to taste with salt and pepper and garnish with the lemon zest.

DESSERTS

Coconut Rice Cake

Servings: 8
Cooking Time: 30 Minutes

Ingredients:

- 1 cup all-natural coconut water
- 1 cup unsweetened coconut milk
- 1 teaspoon almond extract
- ¼ teaspoon salt
- 4 tablespoons honey
- cooking spray
- ¾ cup raw jasmine rice
- 2 cups sliced or cubed fruit

Directions:

1. In a medium bowl, mix together the coconut water, coconut milk, almond extract, salt, and honey.
2. Spray air fryer oven baking pan with cooking spray and add the rice.
3. Pour liquid mixture over rice.
4. Preheat the toaster oven to 360°F and air-fry for 15 minutes. Stir and air-fry for 15 minutes longer or until rice grains are tender.
5. Allow cake to cool slightly. Run a dull knife around edge of cake, inside the pan. Turn the cake out onto a platter and garnish with fruit.

Maple-glazed Pumpkin Pie

Servings: 2
Cooking Time: 10 Minutes

Ingredients:

- Filling:
- 1 15-ounce can pumpkin pie filling
- 1 12-ounce can low-fat evaporated milk
- 1 egg
- 3 tablespoons maple syrup
- ½ teaspoon grated nutmeg
- ½ teaspoon ground ginger
- 1 teaspoon ground cinnamon
- Salt to taste
- 1 Apple Juice Piecrust, baked (recipe follows)
- Dark glaze:
- 3 tablespoons maple syrup
- 2 tablespoons dark brown sugar

Directions:

1. Preheat the toaster oven to 400° F.
2. Combine all the filling ingredients in a large bowl and beat with an electric mixer until smooth. Pour into the piecrust shell.
3. BAKE for 40 minutes, or until a knife inserted in the center comes out clean.
4. Combine the dark glaze ingredients in a baking pan.
5. BROIL for 5 minutes, or until bubbling. Remove from the oven and stir to dissolve the sugar. Broil again for 3 minutes, or until the liquid is thickened and the sugar is dissolved. Spoon on top of the cooled pumpkin pie, spreading evenly, then chill for at least 1 hour before serving.

Mini Gingerbread Bundt Cakes

Servings: 16
Cooking Time: 24 Minutes

Ingredients:

- 3 cups all-purpose flour
- 1/4 cup baking cocoa
- 1 tablespoon baking soda
- 1 teaspoon ground cinnamon

- 1 teaspoon ground ginger
- 1 teaspoon salt
- 1/4 teaspoon ground cloves
- 1/4 teaspoon ground nutmeg
- 1 cup butter, softened
- 1 1/4 cups milk
- 1 cup packed dark brown sugar
- 1 cup molasses
- 2 large eggs
- 1 cup mini chocolate chips Glaze: 1 package (12 oz.) semi-sweet chocolate chips
- 1/3 cup heavy cream
- 2 tablespoons butter
- 2 tablespoons light corn syrup
- Chopped crystallized ginger

Directions:

1. Preheat the toaster oven to 350°F. Spray mini bundt pans with nonstick cooking spray. Dust with flour.

2. In a medium bowl, stir together flour, cocoa, baking soda, cinnamon, ginger, salt, cloves and nutmeg.

3. In a large mixer bowl, beat butter until creamy. Gradually beat in milk, brown sugar, molasses and eggs until well blended.

4. Reduce speed to LOW. Slowly add flour mixture until blended. Stir in chocolate chips.

5. Pour into prepared bundt pans.

6. Bake 20 to 24 minutes or until toothpick inserted in center comes out clean.

7. Cool on wire rack 10 minutes. Invert onto cooling rack and cool completely.

8. In a microwavable bowl, stir together 1 cup chocolate chips, heavy cream, butter and corn syrup.

9. Microwave on MEDIUM power 1 minute or until chips are shiny. Stir until mixture is smooth.

10. Spread glaze over top of each mini bundt and sprinkle with crystallized ginger.

Peanut Butter S'mores

Servings: 10
Cooking Time: 1 Minutes

Ingredients:

- 10 Graham crackers (full, double-square cookies as they come out of the package)
- 5 tablespoons Natural-style creamy or crunchy peanut butter
- ½ cup Milk chocolate chips
- 10 Standard-size marshmallows (not minis and not jumbo campfire ones)

Directions:

1. Preheat the toaster oven to 350°F.

2. Break the graham crackers in half widthwise at the marked place, so the rectangle is now in two squares. Set half of the squares flat side up on your work surface. Spread each with about 1½ teaspoons peanut butter, then set 10 to 12 chocolate chips point side up into the peanut butter on each, pressing gently so the chips stick.

3. Flatten a marshmallow between your clean, dry hands and set it atop the chips. Do the same with the remaining marshmallows on the other coated graham crackers. Do not set the other half of the graham crackers on top of these coated graham crackers.

4. When the machine is at temperature, set the treats graham cracker side down in a single layer in the air fryer oven. They may touch, but even a fraction of an inch between them will provide better air flow. Air-fry undisturbed for 45 seconds.

5. Use a nonstick-safe spatula to transfer the topped graham crackers to a wire rack. Set the other graham cracker squares flat side down over the marshmallows. Cool for a couple of minutes before serving.

Cranapple Crisp

Servings: 6
Cooking Time: 35 Minutes

Ingredients:
- 2 apples, peeled, cored, and diced
- 3 cups chopped fresh or thawed frozen cranberries
- ¼ cup brown sugar
- ¼ cup wheat germ
- 1 tablespoon margarine
- 1 tablespoon vegetable oil
- ½ cup brown sugar
- 1 teaspoon ground cinnamon
- ¼ teaspoon grated nutmeg
- Salt to taste

Directions:
1. Preheat the toaster oven to 350° F.
2. Combine the cranberries, apples, and sugar in a large bowl, mixing well. Transfer to an oiled or nonstick 8½ × 8½ × 2-inch square baking (cake) pan. Set aside.
3. Combine the topping ingredients in a medium bowl, stirring with a fork until crumbly. Sprinkle evenly on top of the cranberry/apple mixture.
4. BAKE for 35 minutes, or until the top is golden brown.

Not Key Lime, Lime Pie

Servings: 3
Cooking Time: 27 Minutes

Ingredients:
- 1 tablespoon grated lime zest
- 3 large egg yolks
- 1 (14-ounce) can sweetened condensed milk
- ½ cup fresh lime juice
- 1 ¾ cups graham cracker crumbs (about 12 full graham crackers)
- ⅓ cup granulated sugar
- ⅛ teaspoon table salt
- ½ cup unsalted butter, melted
- Nonstick cooking spray
- WHIPPED CREAM
- 1 cup heavy cream
- ⅓ cup confectioners' sugar

Directions:
1. Preheat the toaster oven to 350°F.
2. Whisk the lime zest and egg yolks in a large bowl for 1 minute. Whisk in the sweetened condensed milk and lime juice. Set aside to thicken while you prepare the crust.
3. Stir the graham cracker crumbs, granulated sugar, and salt in a medium bowl. Pour the butter over the mixture and mix until combined and moist. Press the crust evenly into the bottom and up the sides of a 9-inch pie plate. Pack tightly using the back of a large spoon. Bake for 10 minutes. Let cool on a cooling rack.
4. When the crust is completely cool, pour the lime filling inside. Bake for 15 to 17 minutes, or until the center is set (it will still jiggle a bit). Allow the pie to cool completely at room temperature. Spray plastic wrap with nonstick cooking spray and place on the pie. Refrigerate for at least 3 hours or overnight.
5. Beat the cream in a large bowl with an electric mixer at medium-high speed until soft peaks form. Add the confectioners' sugar, one tablespoon at a time, and continue to beat until stiff peaks form. Dollop, pipe, or spread the whipped cream over the pie before serving. Refrigerate leftovers for up to 3 days.

Warm Chocolate Fudge Cakes

Servings: 2

Cooking Time: 35 Minutes

Ingredients:

- 6 tablespoons (1¾ ounces) all-purpose flour
- ¼ teaspoon baking powder
- ⅛ teaspoon baking soda
- ⅛ teaspoon table salt
- 2½ ounces bittersweet chocolate (2 ounces chopped, ½ ounce cut into ½-inch pieces)
- ¼ cup whole milk, room temperature
- 3 tablespoons packed light brown sugar
- 2 tablespoons vegetable oil
- 1 large egg, lightly beaten
- ¼ teaspoon vanilla extract

Directions:

1. Adjust toaster oven rack to middle position and preheat the toaster oven to 350 degrees. Grease and flour two 6-ounce ramekins. Whisk flour, baking powder, baking soda, and salt together in bowl.

2. Microwave chopped chocolate and milk in medium bowl at 50 percent power, stirring occasionally, until chocolate is melted and mixture is smooth, 1 to 3 minutes. Stir in sugar until dissolved; let cool slightly. Whisk in oil, egg, and vanilla until combined. Gently whisk in flour mixture until just combined.

3. Divide batter evenly between prepared ramekins and gently tap each ramekin on counter to release air bubbles. Wipe any drops of batter off sides of ramekins. Gently press chocolate pieces evenly into center of each ramekin to submerge in batter. Place ramekins on small rimmed baking sheet and bake cakes until tops are just firm to touch and center is gooey when pierced with toothpick, 10 to 15 minutes. Let cool for 2 to 3 minutes before serving.

Pineapple Tartlets

Servings: 4

Cooking Time: 20 Minutes

Ingredients:

- Vegetable oil
- 6 sheets phyllo pastry
- 1 8-ounce can crushed pineapple, drained
- 3 tablespoons low-fat cottage cheese
- 2 tablespoons orange or pineapple marmalade
- 6 teaspoons concentrated thawed frozen orange juice
- Vanilla frozen yogurt or nonfat whipped topping

Directions:

1. Preheat the toaster oven to 350° F.

2. Brush the pans of a 6-muffin tin with vegetable oil. Lay a phyllo sheet on a clean, flat surface and brush with oil. Fold the sheet into quarters to fit the muffin pan. Repeat the process for the remaining phyllo sheets and pans.

3. BAKE for 5 minutes, or until lightly browned. Remove from the oven and cool.

4. Combine the pineapple, cottage cheese, and marmalade in a small bowl, mixing well. Fill the phyllo shells (in the pans) with equal portions of the mixture. Drizzle 1 teaspoon orange juice concentrate over each.

5. BAKE at 400° F. for 15 minutes, or until the filling is cooked. Cool and remove the tartlets carefully from the muffin pans to dessert dishes. Top with vanilla frozen yogurt or nonfat whipped topping.

Vegan Swedish Cinnamon Rolls (kanelbullar)

Servings: 8
Cooking Time: 18 Minutes

Ingredients:
- Dough
- 1 cup unsweetened almond milk, slightly warm (100°-110°F)
- ¼ cup vegan butter, melted
- 2 tablespoon organic sugar
- 1 teaspoon instant dry yeast
- ½ teaspoon kosher salt
- 2¾ cups all-purpose flour, divided
- Filling
- 6 tablespoons vegan butter, room temperature
- 6 tablespoons organic dark brown sugar
- 1 tablespoon ground cinnamon
- Egg Wash
- 2 tablespoons unsweetened almond milk
- 1 teaspoon agave nectar
- Glaze
- 2 tablespoons unsweetened almond milk
- ½ cup powdered sugar
- ¼ teaspoon vanilla extract
- Swedish pearl sugar, for sprinkling

Directions:
1. Whisk together the almond milk, melted butter, and sugar from the dough ingredients in a large mixing bowl.
2. Sprinkle the yeast into the milk mixture and allow it to bloom for 5 minutes.
3. Add kosher salt and 2¼-cups of flour into the milk and yeast mixture, then mix until well combined.
4. Cover the bowl with a towel or plastic wrap and set in a warm place to rise for 1 hour, or until it doubles in size.
5. Uncover and knead ½-cup all purpose flour into the risen dough. Continue kneading until it just loses its stickiness. You may need to add additional flour.
6. Roll the dough out into a large rectangle, about ½-inch thick. Fix the corners to make sure they are sharp and even.
7. Spread the softened vegan butter from the filling ingredients over the dough and sprinkle evenly with brown sugar and cinnamon.
8. Roll up the dough, forming a log, and pinch the seam closed. Place seam-side down. Trim off any unevenness on either end.
9. Cut the log in half, then divide each half into 8 evenly sized pieces, about 1½-inches thick each.
10. Line the food tray with parchment paper, then place the cinnamon rolls on the tray.
11. Cover with plastic wrap and place in a warm place to rise for 30 minutes.
12. Preheat the toaster Oven to 375°F.
13. Whisk together egg wash ingredients and lightly brush the wash on the tops of the cinnamon rolls.
14. Insert the food tray with the cinnamon rolls at mid position in the preheated oven.
15. Select the Bake function, adjust time to 18 minutes, and press Start/Pause.
16. Remove when done.
17. Whisk together almond milk, powdered sugar, and vanilla extract from the glaze ingredients to make the icing, brush it all over the cinnamon rolls, then sprinkle the rolls with Swedish pearl sugar.
18. Cool before serving, or eat warm.

Heritage Chocolate Chip Cookies

Servings: 16-18
Cooking Time: 12 Minutes

Ingredients:

- 1 1/2 cups all-purpose flour
- 1 teaspoon baking powder
- 1/2 teaspoon salt
- 1 large egg, unbeaten
- 1/2 cup shortening
- 1/2 cup packed dark brown sugar
- 1/4 cup granulated sugar
- 2 teaspoons vanilla extract
- 1 tablespoon milk
- 1 cup chocolate chips

Directions:

1. Preheat the toaster oven to 375ºF.

2. Place all ingredients except chocolate chips in large mixer bowl. With electric mixer on low speed, beat until ingredients are mixed. Gradually increase speed to medium and beat 3 minutes, stopping to scrape bowl as needed.

3. Add chocolate chips and beat on low until blended.

4. Line cookie sheets with parchment paper. Using a small scoop, place 12 scoops of cookie dough about 1-inch apart on parchment.

5. Bake 10 to 12 minutes or until cookies are browned. Slide parchment with baked cookies onto rack to cool. Repeat with remaining dough.

Individual Peach Crisps

Servings: 2
Cooking Time: 60 Minutes

Ingredients:

- 2 tablespoons granulated sugar, divided
- 1 teaspoon lemon juice
- ¼ teaspoon cornstarch
- ⅛ teaspoon table salt, divided
- 1 pound frozen sliced peaches, thawed
- ⅓ cup whole almonds or pecans, chopped fine
- ¼ cup (1¼ ounces) all-purpose flour
- 2 tablespoons packed light brown sugar
- ⅛ teaspoon ground cinnamon
- Pinch ground nutmeg
- 3 tablespoons unsalted butter, melted and cooled

Directions:

1. Adjust toaster oven rack to lowest position and preheat the toaster oven to 425 degrees. Combine 1 tablespoon granulated sugar, lemon juice, cornstarch, and pinch salt in medium bowl. Gently toss peaches with sugar mixture and divide evenly between two 12-ounce ramekins.

2. Combine almonds, flour, brown sugar, cinnamon, nutmeg, remaining pinch salt, and remaining 1 tablespoon granulated sugar in now-empty bowl. Drizzle with melted butter and toss with fork until evenly moistened and mixture forms large chunks with some pea-size pieces throughout. Sprinkle topping evenly over peaches, breaking up any large chunks.

3. Place ramekins on aluminum foil–lined small rimmed baking sheet and bake until filling is bubbling around edges and topping is deep golden brown, 25 to 30 minutes, rotating sheet halfway through baking. Let crisps cool on wire rack for 15 minutes before serving.

Meringue Topping

Servings: 1

Cooking Time: 12 Minutes

Ingredients:

- 3 egg whites
- 1 cup sugar

Directions:

1. Beat the egg whites and sugar together in a medium bowl until the mixture is stiff. Spread on top of the pie.
2. BAKE at 375°F. for 12 minutes, or until the meringue topping is browned.

Make-ahead Oatmeal-raisin Cookies

Servings: 8

Cooking Time: 45 Minutes

Ingredients:

- 1 cup (5 ounces) all-purpose flour
- ¾ teaspoon table salt
- ½ teaspoon baking soda
- ¼ teaspoon ground cinnamon
- ¾ cup (5¼ ounces) dark brown sugar
- ½ cup (3½ ounces) granulated sugar
- ½ cup vegetable oil
- 4 tablespoons unsalted butter, melted and cooled
- 1 large egg plus 1 large yolk
- 1 teaspoon vanilla extract
- 3 cups (9 ounces) old-fashioned rolled oats
- ½ cup raisins

Directions:

1. Adjust toaster oven rack to middle position and preheat the toaster oven to 350 degrees. Line large and small rimmed baking sheets with parchment paper. Whisk flour, salt, baking soda, and cinnamon together in bowl.
2. Whisk brown sugar and granulated sugar together in medium bowl. Whisk in oil and melted butter until combined. Whisk in egg and yolk and vanilla until smooth. Gently stir in flour mixture with rubber spatula until soft dough forms. Fold in oats and raisins until evenly distributed (mixture will be stiff).
3. Working with 3 tablespoons dough at a time, roll into balls. Space desired number of dough balls at least 1½ inches apart on prepared small sheet; space remaining dough balls evenly on prepared large sheet. Using bottom of greased dry measuring cup, press each ball until 2½ inches in diameter.
4. Bake small sheet of cookies until edges are just beginning to brown and centers are still soft but not wet, 10 to 15 minutes. Let cookies cool slightly on sheet. Serve warm or at room temperature.
5. Freeze remaining large sheet of cookies until firm, about 1 hour. Transfer cookies to 1-gallon zipper-lock bag and freeze for up to 1 month. Bake frozen cookies as directed; do not thaw.

Honey-roasted Mixed Nuts

Servings: 8

Cooking Time: 15 Minutes

Ingredients:

- ½ cup raw, shelled pistachios
- ½ cup raw almonds
- 1 cup raw walnuts
- 2 tablespoons filtered water
- 2 tablespoons honey
- 1 tablespoon vegetable oil
- 2 tablespoons sugar

- ½ teaspoon salt

Directions:

1. Preheat the toaster oven to 300°F.

2. Lightly spray an air-fryer-safe pan with olive oil; then place the pistachios, almonds, and walnuts inside the pan and place the pan inside the air fryer oven.

3. Air-fry for 15 minutes, every 5 minutes to rotate the nuts.

4. While the nuts are roasting, boil the water in a small pan and stir in the honey and oil. Continue to stir while cooking until the water begins to evaporate and a thick sauce is formed. The sauce should stick to the back of a wooden spoon when mixed. Turn off the heat.

5. Remove the nuts from the air fryer oven (cooking should have just completed) and spoon the nuts into the stovetop pan. Use a spatula to coat the nuts with the honey syrup.

6. Line a baking sheet with parchment paper and spoon the nuts onto the sheet. Lightly sprinkle the sugar and salt over the nuts and let cool in the refrigerator for at least 2 hours.

7. When the honey and sugar have hardened, store the nuts in an airtight container in the refrigerator.

Hasselback Apple Crisp

Servings: 4

Cooking Time: 20 Minutes

Ingredients:

- 2 large Gala apples, peeled, cored and cut in half
- ¼ cup butter, melted
- ½ teaspoon ground cinnamon
- 2 tablespoons sugar
- Topping
- 3 tablespoons butter, melted
- 2 tablespoons brown sugar
- ¼ cup chopped pecans
- 2 tablespoons rolled oats
- 1 tablespoon flour
- vanilla ice cream
- caramel sauce

Directions:

1. Place the apples cut side down on a cutting board. Slicing from stem end to blossom end, make 8 to 10 slits down the apple halves but only slice three quarters of the way through the apple, not all the way through to the cutting board.

2. Preheat the toaster oven to 330°F and pour a little water into the bottom of the air fryer oven drawer. (This will help prevent the grease that drips into the bottom drawer from burning and smoking.)

3. Transfer the apples to the air fryer oven, flat side down. Combine ¼ cup of melted butter, cinnamon and sugar in a small bowl. Brush this butter mixture onto the apples and air-fry at 330°F for 15 minutes. Baste the apples several times with the butter mixture during the cooking process.

4. While the apples are air-frying, make the filling. Combine 3 tablespoons of melted butter with the brown sugar, pecans, rolled oats and flour in a bowl. Stir with a fork until the mixture resembles small crumbles.

5. When the timer on the air fryer oven is up, spoon the topping down the center of the apples. Air-fry at 330°F for an additional 5 minutes.

6. Transfer the apples to a serving plate and serve with vanilla ice cream and caramel sauce.

Pear And Almond Biscotti Crumble

Servings: 6
Cooking Time: 65 Minutes

Ingredients:

- 7-inch cake pan or ceramic dish
- 3 pears, peeled, cored and sliced
- ½ cup brown sugar
- ¼ teaspoon ground ginger
- 1 teaspoon ground cinnamon
- ⅛ teaspoon ground nutmeg
- 2 tablespoons cornstarch
- 1¼ cups (4 to 5) almond biscotti, coarsely crushed
- ¼ cup all-purpose flour
- ¼ cup sliced almonds
- ¼ cup butter, melted

Directions:

1. Combine the pears, brown sugar, ginger, cinnamon, nutmeg and cornstarch in a bowl. Toss to combine and then pour the pear mixture into a greased 7-inch cake pan or ceramic dish.
2. Combine the crushed biscotti, flour, almonds and melted butter in a medium bowl. Toss with a fork until the mixture resembles large crumbles. Sprinkle the biscotti crumble over the pears and cover the pan with aluminum foil.
3. Preheat the toaster oven to 350°F.
4. Air-fry at 350°F for 60 minutes. Remove the aluminum foil and air-fry for an additional 5 minutes to brown the crumble layer.
5. Serve warm.

Spice Cake

Servings: 6
Cooking Time: 25 Minutes

Ingredients:

- 1 cup applesauce or 2 4-ounce jars baby food prunes
- ¼ cup skim milk or low-fat soy milk
- 1 tablespoon vegetable oil
- ½ cup brown sugar
- 1 egg
- 1½ cups unbleached flour
- 1 teaspoon baking powder
- ½ teaspoon baking soda
- ¼ teaspoon grated nutmeg
- ½ teaspoon ground cinnamon
- ½ teaspoon grated orange zest
- Salt to taste
- Creamy Frosting

Directions:

1. Preheat the toaster oven to 350° F.
2. Stir together the applesauce, milk, oil, sugar, and egg in a small bowl. Set aside.
3. Combine the flour, baking powder, nutmeg, cinnamon, orange zest, and salt in a medium bowl. Add the applesauce mixture and stir to mix well. Pour the batter into an oiled or nonstick 8½ × 8½ × 2-inch square baking (cake) pan.
4. BAKE for 25 minutes, or until a toothpick inserted in the center comes out clean. Frost with Creamy Frosting.

Cheese Blintzes

Servings: 6
Cooking Time: 10 Minutes

Ingredients:

- 1½ 7½-ounce package(s) farmer cheese
- 3 tablespoons Regular or low-fat cream cheese (not fat-free)
- 3 tablespoons Granulated white sugar
- ¼ teaspoon Vanilla extract

- 6 Egg roll wrappers
- 3 tablespoons Butter, melted and cooled

Directions:

1. Preheat the toaster oven to 375°F.
2. Use a flatware fork to mash the farmer cheese, cream cheese, sugar, and vanilla in a small bowl until smooth.
3. Set one egg roll wrapper on a clean, dry work surface. Place ¼ cup of the filling at the edge closest to you, leaving a ½-inch gap before the edge of the wrapper. Dip your clean finger in water and wet the edges of the wrapper. Fold the perpendicular sides over the filling, then roll the wrapper closed with the filling inside. Set it aside seam side down and continue filling the remainder of the wrappers.
4. Brush the wrappers on all sides with the melted butter. Be generous. Set them seam side down in the air fryer oven with as much space between them as possible. Air-fry undisturbed for 10 minutes, or until lightly browned.
5. Use a nonstick-safe spatula to transfer the blintzes to a wire rack. Cool for at least 5 minutes or up to 20 minutes before serving.

Giant Oatmeal–peanut Butter Cookie

Servings: 4
Cooking Time: 18 Minutes

Ingredients:

- 1 cup Rolled oats (not quick-cooking or steel-cut oats)
- ½ cup All-purpose flour
- ½ teaspoon Ground cinnamon
- ½ teaspoon Baking soda
- ⅓ cup Packed light brown sugar
- ¼ cup Solid vegetable shortening
- 2 tablespoons Natural-style creamy peanut butter
- 3 tablespoons Granulated white sugar
- 2 tablespoons (or 1 small egg, well beaten) Pasteurized egg substitute, such as Egg Beaters
- ⅓ cup Roasted, salted peanuts, chopped
- Baking spray

Directions:

1. Preheat the toaster oven to 350°F..
2. Stir the oats, flour, cinnamon, and baking soda in a bowl until well combined.
3. Using an electric hand mixer at medium speed, beat the brown sugar, shortening, peanut butter, granulated white sugar, and egg substitute or egg (as applicable) until smooth and creamy, about 3 minutes, scraping down the inside of the bowl occasionally.
4. Scrape down and remove the beaters. Fold in the flour mixture and peanuts with a rubber spatula just until all the flour is moistened and the peanut bits are evenly distributed in the dough.
5. For a small air fryer oven, coat the inside of a 6-inch round cake pan with baking spray. For a medium air fryer oven, coat the inside of a 7-inch round cake pan with baking spray. And for a large air fryer oven, coat the inside of an 8-inch round cake pan with baking spray. Scrape and gently press the dough into the prepared pan, spreading it into an even layer to the perimeter.
6. Set the pan in the air fryer oven and air-fry undisturbed for 18 minutes, or until well browned.
7. Transfer the pan to a wire rack and cool for 15 minutes. Loosen the cookie from the perimeter with a spatula, then invert the pan onto a cutting board and let the cookie come free. Remove the pan and reinvert the cookie onto the wire rack. Cool for 5 minutes more before slicing into wedges to serve.

Rum-glazed Roasted Pineapple

Servings: 4
Cooking Time: 45 Minutes

Ingredients:

- ½ pineapple, peeled, cored, and cut lengthwise into 4 wedges
- 2 tablespoons unsalted butter, melted
- 3 tablespoons packed dark brown sugar
- 1 tablespoon lime juice
- ½ teaspoon vanilla extract
- Pinch table salt
- 1 tablespoon white or aged rum
- 2 tablespoons unsweetened shredded coconut, toasted

Directions:

1. Adjust toaster oven rack to lowest position and preheat the toaster oven to 450 degrees. Toss pineapple with melted butter in 8-inch square baking dish or pan, then arrange in single layer. Roast until bottoms of wedges are deep golden brown and fork slips easily in and out of pineapple, 25 to 35 minutes, rotating dish halfway through roasting.

2. Remove pan from oven and transfer pineapple to serving dish. Whisk sugar, lime juice, vanilla, and salt into butter and juice in pan, scraping up any browned bits, until well combined. Return pineapple wedges to pan, browned side up, along with any accumulated juices. Roast until sauce is reduced to syrupy consistency, 3 to 5 minutes.

3. Remove pan from oven and transfer pineapple to serving dish. Whisk rum into sauce in pan until smooth, then spoon sauce over pineapple. Sprinkle with coconut and serve.

German Chocolate Cake

Servings: 6

Cooking Time: 25 Minutes

Ingredients:

- Butter, shortening, or nonstick cooking spray
- ⅔ cup whole milk
- ½ teaspoon white vinegar
- ⅔ cup all-purpose flour
- 3 tablespoons unsweetened cocoa powder
- ½ teaspoon baking soda
- ½ teaspoon baking powder
- ¼ teaspoon table salt
- ½ cup packed dark brown sugar
- 2 tablespoons canola or vegetable oil
- 1 large egg
- ½ teaspoon pure vanilla extract
- GERMAN CHOCOLATE FROSTING
- 1 large egg yolk
- ½ cup evaporated milk
- ⅓ cup granulated sugar
- 3 tablespoons unsalted butter
- ¾ cup sweetened flaked coconut
- ⅓ cup chopped pecans, toasted

Directions:

1. Preheat the toaster oven to 350°F. Line an 8-inch round cake pan with parchment paper and lightly grease the bottom and sides with butter or shortening or spray with nonstick cooking spray.

2. Pour the milk into a medium bowl and stir in the vinegar; set aside.

3. Whisk the flour, cocoa, baking soda, baking powder, and salt in a small bowl; set aside.

4. Whisk the brown sugar, oil, egg, and vanilla in a medium bowl. Add the flour mixture, in thirds, alternately with the milk mixture, beginning and ending with the flour. Blend well and scrape the sides of the bowl as needed.

5. Pour the batter into the prepared pan. Bake for 20 to 25 minutes, or until a wooden pick

inserted into the center comes out clean. Let cool on a wire rack for 10 minutes. Invert onto a serving platter and allow to cool completely.

6. Make the frosting: Combine the egg yolk, evaporated milk, sugar, and butter in a small saucepan. Cook, stirring, over medium heat for about 6 minutes or until thickened and bubbly. Remove from the heat and stir in the coconut and pecans. Cover and let cool completely. Frost the top of the cake.

Key Lime Pie

Servings: 8
Cooking Time: 60 Minutes

Ingredients:
- FILLING
- 1 (14-ounce) can sweetened condensed milk
- 4 large egg yolks
- 4 teaspoons grated lime zest plus ½ cup juice (5 limes)
- CRUST
- 11 whole graham crackers, broken into 1-inch pieces
- 3 tablespoons granulated sugar
- 5 tablespoons unsalted butter, melted and cooled
- TOPPING
- ¾ cup heavy cream
- ¼ cup (1 ounce) confectioners' sugar

Directions:
1. FOR THE FILLING: Whisk condensed milk, egg yolks, and lime zest and juice together in bowl until smooth. Cover mixture and let sit at room temperature until thickened, about 30 minutes.

2. FOR THE CRUST: Adjust toaster oven rack to middle position and preheat the toaster oven to 325 degrees. Process graham cracker pieces and sugar in food processor to fine, even crumbs, about 30 seconds. Sprinkle melted butter over crumbs and pulse to incorporate, about 5 pulses.

3. Sprinkle mixture into 9-inch pie plate. Using bottom of dry measuring cup, press crumbs into even layer on bottom and up sides of pie plate. Bake until crust is fragrant and beginning to brown, 10 to 15 minutes. Transfer to wire rack and let cool slightly, about 10 minutes.

4. Pour thickened filling into warm crust and smooth top. Bake pie until center is firm but jiggles slightly when shaken, 12 to 17 minutes. Let pie cool slightly on wire rack, about 1 hour. Cover pie loosely with plastic wrap and refrigerate until filling is chilled and set, at least 3 hours or up to 24 hours.

5. For the topping Using stand mixer fitted with whisk attachment, whip cream and sugar on medium-low speed until foamy, about 1 minute. Increase speed to high and whip until soft peaks form, 1 to 3 minutes. (Topping can be refrigerated in fine-mesh strainer set over small bowl and covered with plastic wrap for up to 8 hours.) Spread whipped cream attractively over pie. Serve.

Peanut Butter Cup Doughnut Holes

Servings: 24
Cooking Time: 4 Minutes

Ingredients:
- 1½ cups bread flour
- 1 teaspoon active dry yeast
- 1 tablespoon sugar
- ¼ teaspoon salt
- ½ cup warm milk

- ½ teaspoon vanilla extract
- 2 egg yolks
- 2 tablespoons melted butter
- 24 miniature peanut butter cups, plus a few more for garnish
- vegetable oil, in a spray bottle
- Doughnut Topping
- 1 cup chocolate chips
- 2 tablespoons milk

Directions:

1. Combine the flour, yeast, sugar and salt in a bowl. Add the milk, vanilla, egg yolks and butter. Mix well until the dough starts to come together. Transfer the dough to a floured surface and knead by hand for 2 minutes. Shape the dough into a ball and transfer it to a large oiled bowl. Cover the bowl with a towel and let the dough rise in a warm place for 1 to 1½ hours, until the dough has doubled in size.

2. When the dough has risen, punch it down and roll it into a 24-inch long log. Cut the dough into 24 pieces. Push a peanut butter cup into the center of each piece of dough, pinch the dough shut and roll it into a ball. Place the dough balls on a cookie sheet and let them rise in a warm place for 30 minutes.

3. Preheat the toaster oven to 400°F.

4. Spray or brush the dough balls lightly with vegetable oil. Air-fry eight at a time, at 400°F for 4 minutes, turning them over halfway through the cooking process.

5. While the doughnuts are air frying, prepare the topping. Place the chocolate chips and milk in a microwave safe bowl. Microwave on high for 1 minute. Stir and microwave for an additional 30 seconds if necessary to get all the chips to melt. Stir until the chips are melted and smooth.

6. Dip the top half of the doughnut holes into the melted chocolate. Place them on a rack to set up for just a few minutes and watch them disappear.

Chocolate Caramel Pecan Cupcakes

Servings: 6
Cooking Time: 20 Minutes

Ingredients:

- 6 tablespoons all-purpose flour
- 6 tablespoons unsweetened cocoa powder
- ¼ teaspoon baking soda
- ¼ teaspoon baking powder
- ⅛ teaspoon table salt
- 6 tablespoons unsalted butter, softened
- ½ cup granulated sugar
- 1 large egg
- ½ teaspoon pure vanilla extract
- ½ cup sour cream
- BUTTERCREAM FROSTING
- ¼ cup unsalted butter, softened
- 1 ¾ cups confectioners' sugar
- 2 to 3 tablespoons half-and-half or milk
- 1 teaspoon pure vanilla extract
- Caramel ice cream topping
- ¼ cup caramelized chopped pecans

Directions:

1. Preheat the toaster oven to 350°F. Line a 6-cup muffin pan with cupcake papers.

2. Whisk the flour, cocoa, baking soda, baking powder, and salt in a small bowl; set aside.

3. Beat the butter and granulated sugar in a large bowl with a handheld mixer at medium-high speed for 2 minutes, or until the mixture is light and creamy. Beat in the egg well. Beat in the vanilla.

4. On low speed, beat in the flour mixture in thirds, alternating with the sour cream, beginning and ending with the flour mixture. The batter will be thick.

5. Spoon the batter evenly into the prepared cupcake cups, filling each about three-quarters full. Bake for 18 to 20 minutes, or until a wooden pick inserted into the center comes out clean. Place on a wire rack and let cool completely.

6. Meanwhile, make the frosting: Beat the butter in a large bowl using a handheld mixer on medium-high speed until creamy. Gradually beat in the confectioners' sugar. Beat in 2 tablespoons of half-and-half and the vanilla. Beat in the remaining tablespoon of half-and-half, as needed, until the frosting is of desired consistency.

7. Frost each cooled cupcake. Drizzle the caramel topping in thin, decorative stripes over the frosting. Top with the caramelized pecans.

Apple Strudel

Servings: 2

Cooking Time: 90 Minutes

Ingredients:

- 2 Golden Delicious apples (14 ounces), peeled, cored, and cut into ½-inch pieces
- 1½ tablespoons granulated sugar
- ¼ teaspoon grated lemon zest plus 1 teaspoon juice
- ⅛ teaspoon ground cinnamon
- ⅛ teaspoon ground ginger
- ⅛ teaspoon table salt, divided
- 2 tablespoons golden raisins
- 1 tablespoon panko bread crumbs
- 3½ tablespoons unsalted butter, melted
- 1½ teaspoons confectioners' sugar, plus extra for serving
- 7 (14 by 9-inch) phyllo sheets, thawed

Directions:

1. Toss apples, granulated sugar, lemon zest and juice, cinnamon, ginger, and pinch salt together in large bowl. Cover and microwave until apples are softened, 2 to 4 minutes, stirring once halfway through microwaving. Let apples sit, covered, for 5 minutes. Transfer apples to colander set in second large bowl and let drain, reserving liquid. Return apples to bowl; stir in raisins and panko.

2. Adjust toaster oven rack to middle position and preheat the toaster oven to 350 degrees. Spray small rimmed baking sheet with vegetable oil spray. Stir remaining pinch salt into melted butter.

3. Place 16½ by 12-inch sheet of parchment paper on counter with long side parallel to edge of counter. Place 1 phyllo sheet on parchment with long side parallel to edge of counter. Place confectioners' sugar in fine-mesh strainer. Lightly brush sheet with melted butter and dust sparingly with confectioners' sugar. Repeat with remaining 6 phyllo sheets, melted butter, and confectioners' sugar, stacking sheets one on top of other as you go.

4. Arrange apple mixture in 2½ by 10-inch rectangle 2 inches from bottom of phyllo and about 2 inches from each side. Using parchment, fold sides of phyllo over filling, then fold bottom edge of phyllo over filling. Brush folded portions of phyllo with reserved apple liquid. Fold top edge over filling, making sure top and bottom edges overlap by about 1 inch. (If they do not

overlap, unfold, rearrange filling into slightly narrower strip, and refold.) Press firmly to seal. Using thin metal spatula, transfer strudel to prepared sheet. Lightly brush top and sides of strudel with remaining apple liquid.

5. Bake until golden brown, 25 to 30 minutes, rotating sheet halfway through baking. Using thin metal spatula, immediately transfer strudel to cutting board. Let cool for 3 minutes. Slice strudel and let cool for at least 20 minutes. Serve warm or at room temperature, dusting with extra confectioners' sugar before serving.

RECIPE INDEX

Classic Tuna Casserole 44
Coconut Chicken With Apricot-ginger Sauce 55
Coconut Rice Cake 105
Crab-stuffed Peppers 34
Cranapple Crisp 107
Creamy Parmesan Polenta 80
Creamy Roasted Pepper Basil Soup 42
Creamy Scalloped Potatoes 81
Crisp Cajun Potato Wedges 103
Crispy Calamari 32
Crispy Chicken Parmesan 64
Crispy Chicken Tenders 53
Crispy Fried Onion Chicken Breasts 59
Crispy Tofu Bites 86
Crunchy And Buttery Cod With Ritz® Cracker Crust 35
Crunchy Roasted Potatoes 94
Curry Powder 57

E

Eggplant And Tomato Slices 100
Extra Crispy Country-style Pork Riblets 68

F

Fiery Bacon-wrapped Dates 91
Fiesta Chicken Plate 58
Fish And "chips" 39
Fried Apple Wedges 86
Fried Chicken 59
Fried Shrimp 33
Fry Bread 21

G

Gardener's Rice 47
German Chocolate Cake 115
Giant Oatmeal–peanut Butter Cookie 114
Ginger Miso Calamari 28
Glazed Pork Tenderloin With Carrots Sheet Pan Supper 48

Golden Grilled Cheese Tomato Sandwich 95
Golden Seasoned Chicken Wings 60
Good Stuff Bread 26
Grilled Ham & Muenster Cheese On Raisin Bread 88
Grits Casserole 102
Guiltless Bacon 58

H

Ham And Cheese Palmiers 90
Hashbrown Potatoes Lyonnaise 15
Hasselback Apple Crisp 112
Healthy Southwest Stuffed Peppers 44
Herbed Lamb Burgers 69
Heritage Chocolate Chip Cookies 110
Home Fries 98
Honey Lemon Thyme Glazed Cornish Hen 61
Honey-roasted Mixed Nuts 111
Horseradish-crusted Salmon Fillets 36

I

Indian Fry Bread Tacos 70
Individual Peach Crisps 110
Inspirational Personal Pizza 51
Italian Baked Chicken 64
Italian Baked Stuffed Tomatoes 51
Italian Sausage & Peppers 67

K

Key Lime Pie 116
Kielbasa Chunks With Pineapple & Peppers 71

L

Lamb Burger With Feta And Olives 77
Lemon-dill Salmon Burgers 30
Lentil And Carrot Soup 46
Lentil-stuffed Zucchini 96
Light Beef Stroganoff 48
Light Trout Amandine 29
Lima Bean And Artichoke Casserole 47

Sheet Pan Loaded Nachos 45
Shrimp & Grits 38
Shrimp Patties 29
Skewered Salsa Verde Shrimp 34
Slow Cooked Carnitas 66
Slow Cooker Chicken Philly Cheesesteak
Sandwich 47
Smoked Gouda Bacon Macaroni And Cheese 91
Snapper With Capers And Olives 28
Soft Pretzels 24
Southern-style Biscuits 14
Spice Cake 113
Spice-rubbed Split Game Hen 64
Spicy Oven-baked Chili 45
Steak Pinwheels With Pepper Slaw And
Minneapolis Potato Salad 71
Steak With Herbed Butter 76
Strawberry Toast 18
Stuffed Bell Peppers 73
Sugar-glazed Walnuts 84
Sweet Chili Shrimp 32

Sweet Potato Casserole 83

T
Tex-mex Fish Tacos 34
Traditional Pot Roast 72
Turkey And Tuna Melt 14
Tuscan Pork Tenderloin 74

V
Vegan Swedish Cinnamon Rolls (kanelbullar)
109
Vietnamese Beef Lettuce Wraps 74

W
Warm And Salty Edamame 83
Warm Chocolate Fudge Cakes 108

Y
Yeast Dough For Two Pizzas 45
Yellow Squash 97

Z
Zesty London Broil 72

Printed by Libri Plureos GmbH in Hamburg, Germany